DRIVE
TO THE
TOP!

*5 Timeless Business
Lessons Learned from
Golf's Greatest
Champions*

DR. RICK JENSEN

Cover design by David Marty
Text layout by Ethan Evanston

Sea Script Company
Seattle, Washington

ISBN: 978-0-9785436-6-2
Library of Congress Card Catalogue No.: 2007940387

First Printing January 2008
Second Printing November 2009

Printed in Hong Kong

For more information, visit:
www.drrickjensen.com

SEA   SCRIPT   COMPANY
www.seascriptcompany.com
info@seascriptcompany.com
206.748.0345

TABLE OF CONTENTS

What character traits do champions like Tiger Woods and Jack Nicklaus have in common? How can you develop those same traits and use them to become the best at what you do?

Are you truly passionate about your pursuits? Take the time to explore your interests, work values, and skills as you define specific goals that will take your performance to the next level. Champions love what they do—and so should you!

Top golfers have the rare ability to identify the essential drivers of results in their field of play. Learn how to identify the essentials in your business and concentrate your efforts where they'll have the greatest impact on getting the results you want.

To identify their own relative strengths and weakness, touring golf pros are constantly benchmarking themselves against the likes of Tiger Woods and Annika Sorenstam. Who are the Tigers and Annikas of your world? How do you measure up to them?

Now let's get inside the ropes of the PGA and LPGA tours and see how world-class golfers train to become the best. By applying these same training techniques in your work, you can create an action plan to address your greatest, most essential needs.

You can call it implementation, execution, or walking the talk—in business and in golf, champions take their new knowledge "to-the-course," where it will pay off in real results.

This book can be more than a pleasant, thought-provoking read. It can and should become your personal action plan for taking that next immediate step toward fulfilling your dreams. You've taken the time to write down your insights, aspirations, and strategies throughout this book. Now—use it before you lose it!

Scott McNealy
Chairman and Co-Founder
Sun Microsystems

Dr. Rick Jensen asked me to write a foreword to his book most likely because two of my greatest passions—business and golf (and not necessarily in that order)—also happen to be two of his.

For me, as for Dr. Rick, those two passions have also been long intertwined.

As a boy, some of my happiest memories are of playing golf and talking business with my dad, Raymond William McNealy, an American Motors executive. One time our foursome included another pretty solid golfer and business executive, Lee Iacocca. I was all eyes and ears!

While attending Harvard, I made the golf team and became its captain. Later in business, golf remained a big part of my life. In 1998, I was recognized by *Golf Digest* magazine as the top ranked golfer among CEOs, a position that I proudly held for a few years. At one point, I was ranked #1, and Jack Welch, the legendary CEO of General Electric and a longtime business hero of mine, was ranked #2. Though GE was already a customer of Sun Microsystems, I'd never met Jack, so I used our rankings as an opportunity to introduce myself. Knowing what a competitive guy he is, I challenged him to a game—any time, any place, *mano a mano*.

Jack won our first couple of matches, but I won the last. The upshot was that I not only got the opportunity to meet Jack but to know him pretty well. As Dr. Rick asserts, you must "surround yourself with winners," and who better than Jack Welch. I've learned a lot about business (and maybe even a little about golf) from him. At Jack's urging I later joined GE's Board of Directors.

As Dr. Rick shows throughout this book, there are many useful lessons that those of us in business can learn from the disciplined habits of golf's great champions. One that really resonates with me is what Dr. Rick calls "calculated risk-taking." At Sun Microsystems, our team knows that it is okay to take risks. Risk-taking is what drives innovation, and without it there would never have been a Sun Microsystems in the first place.

My energies are always focused on identifying, measuring, and developing those factors that most drive results. As you read *Drive to the Top*, Dr. Rick outlines five essential steps that will help you do the same—in business, and yes, in golf as well.

My work is tremendously rewarding and I wouldn't trade it for anything in the world, even a spot on the PGA Tour.

On the other hand, if I could have a 15-footer on #18 at Augusta to win the Masters...

ACKNOWLEDGEMENTS

First I'd like to thank the "foursome" who helped make this book a reality.

Greg Daugherty—the best! Phenomenal writer/editor, with great ability to capture my voice and help me express my thoughts more clearly. For someone who primarily speaks for a living, it is invaluable to have someone so masterful in converting the spoken word into book form for others to read and enjoy.

Lorin Anderson—a great friend and colleague who has worn more hats in the process of this book project than one could collect on a hat rack. He's been a confidant, mentor, coach, guide, business partner, editor, visionary, and marketing genius. Lorin has been instrumental in taking this book from an idea and getting it done!

Marilyn Allen—my literary agent, who has all the answers. Great to have a "one stop shop" when it comes to what it takes to get a book written, published, distributed, you name it.

Beth Farrell—publisher, for her invaluable input on the logistics involved in the design, layout, production, and publishing of this book. Wonderfully responsive, helpful, knowledgeable, flexible.

I'm also thankful to all of those individuals in business management who have provided invaluable input, guidance, knowledge, and application as we have worked closely to apply the performance essentials discussed in this book where it matters—in the field! Thank you to: Steve Weiner, Jim Gallagher, Mark Kiniry, Pat Murphy, Wayne Badorf, Phillip Trimble, Jayne Rodenkirk, Keith Burger, Todd Kimmelman, Maureen Ehrenberg, Doug Frye, Mike Levinson, Jorge Gonzalez, Peter Morrice, and Bill Hicks.

To all the business professionals, wholesalers, real estate agents, marketing teams, sales teams, and administrative staff, who have provided insights, experiences, case studies, knowledge, and hours of informative dialogue, teaching me what they know and how they apply it. They have helped me learn, expand my own horizons, and communicate their successes and strategies to others. Specifically I'd like to thank John Marshall, Corrie Wilder, Mason Hughes, Chris Cooke, and Brian Cooke for their direct contributions (case examples) to the text of this book.

On the golf side, I am very appreciative of the support that I have received over the past 15 years from the management and staff of PGA National Resort and Spa. Additionally, I owe special thanks to the many professionals and coaches who have contributed their time, energy, knowledge, and enthusiasm. My work with touring pros, aspiring pros, club pros, teaching pros, as well as the corporate golfer, would never be possible without all the ideas, techniques, and strategies that I have "borrowed" from them over the years. And, oh yes, thanks for the endless golf tips they have provided me in an effort to bring my personal golf game to a level worthy of stepping on the same tee with each of them. Thank you to: Rick Martino, Mike McGetrick, Butch Harmon, Jr., David Leadbetter, Chuck Cook, Martin Hall, Rick McCord, Dick Farley, Mike Adams, Charlie King, Craig Shankland, Bob Percey, Cindy Ferro, Mike Bender, Cheryl Anderson,

Craig Harmon, Laird Small, Carol Mann, Henry Brunton, Tom Patri, Bill Davis, Jackie Cannizzo, Patrick Leahy, Randy Smith, Buddy Alexander, Mimi Ryan, Carolyn O'Connor, Kevin Marsh, Rick Whitfield, Jeff Roth, Brian Peaper, Bill Moretti, Nancy Quarcelino, Todd Anderson, Randy Myers, John Gardner, Dom DiJulia, Mike Davis, Kevin Walker, Todd Sones, Michael Breed, David Glenz, Charlie Sorrell, Eden Foster, Peter Krause, Hank Johnson, and Dr. Jim Suttie.

Finally, to some other dear friends, colleagues, and family.

Ami Tully—If you've ever met someone in your life that you know you were destined to work with, Ami's that person—thoughtful, intelligent, committed, expressive, giving, patient, and most importantly, striving to make a difference! Ami has spent countless hours bringing me up to speed on the "essentials of selling."

John Lotka—John's understanding of how to position ideas in the marketplace and market them to those who matter is phenomenal. His insights have been invaluable in helping me package and organize my thoughts, and deliver them to clients.

Scott McNealy—Thanks to Scott McNealy for epitomizing the principles outlined in this book. Scott's application of the five essentials in both his business and golf endeavors is living proof that what works in business also works in golf.

Bruce Johnston—I've known Bruce for 10 years, and he has allowed me the opportunity to field test my ideas across corporate America while providing invaluable input as to how I can better influence business professionals. Bruce has been the utmost supporter of the ideas discussed in this book, and he has been instrumental in turning these ideas into tangible programs and materials that have a positive impact on advisors, wholesalers, and sales growth in the world of financial services.

George Endres—Pronounced "end—res," as I am too often in need of reminding. George, the father to two wonderful golfers as well as a manager in the world of financial services, has been a consistent sounding board for me. Our conversations in the boardroom and on the golf course have led to many ideas that have materialized in this book.

Cara Peck—Cara has been influential in pushing me to develop and deliver information that can be retained, embraced, and put to use immediately in the field. As a manager and a communicator, Cara is living proof that "character" is the driving force behind an individual's success.

Matt Lobas—As he has worked diligently improving his grip on the golf course, Matt has worked even harder to build training platforms and resources that are invaluable to his sales team and their clients. Matt's ability to put ideas into action has been vital in pushing me to develop materials and tools that move my information from concept to applied tools.

Leslie Hunnicutt—Leslie has taken a leadership role in applying the principles outlined in the book specifically to her team and the clients that they serve. She has allowed me the opportunity to create materials that take these principles to the field where they can have real, measurable benefit.

Scott McKain—a trusted colleague and a most impressive author and speaker in the arena of enhancing the customer experience. Scott's wonderful creativity and forward thinking continually challenge me to take my material and delivery to the next level.

Jim Gerber—My good friend, who epitomizes the golf professional who truly understands and practices the business concepts expressed in this book. We've had lengthy discussions in golf and business venues around the country discussing the commonalities between the worlds of golf and business. Jim willingness to include me in many of his corporate golf ventures, as well as our discussions led to many of the concepts expressed in this book.

Eric Frasier—Eric epitomizes the ideas of "focusing on what's essential," and he has truly "taken it to the course" in his efforts to apply the essential performance principles discussed in this book to his work in financial services. Eric has spent countless hours educating me about the world of financial services and the essentials of wholesaling—information that has been invaluable as I've worked to apply my teachings in this industry.

Len Travaglione—My good friend, who has supported and advised me since we were in graduate school together. Len was there at the genesis of this book, at the Venetian Hotel, which resulted in the initial outline and clarification for the five essentials discussed in this book. My appreciation for his ongoing support, patience, and encouragement is beyond words.

My parents, Barbara and Ron Jensen, who have unconditionally supported me throughout my life. Their willingness to allow me to speak my mind, have a voice, ask questions, and express my opinions set the stage for my desire to make a difference and my willingness to express my own thoughts.

My wife, Rosemarie, and my kids, Danielle and Connor, for their love, support, and encouragement. They are the most important part of my life. They keep me in check and balanced when my love for my professional pursuits gets the best of me. As my kids have said on many occasions, "Dad, step away from the computer—let's play!"

THIS BOOK IS DEDICATED TO MY "CHILLINS"—DANIELLE AND CONNOR
I LOVE YOU.
"CHILLINS FIRST!"

Introduction

Dr. Rick Jensen

I love my work. Over the past 15 years, I've had the pleasure of coaching and studying many of the top performers in the worlds of sport and business. I've worked with these champions in the locker room, in the boardroom, during competition, during sales calls, on the golf course, and on the job—all the time, intrigued by one question. How do they perform at such a consistently high level?

As a sports psychologist and consultant to such peak performers, I've devoted much of my career to understanding how a champion becomes a champion. Is it genetic? Is it learned? Is it luck? Is it some fortunate combination of all these? Understanding what drives someone to greatness is my passion.

As you read this book, you will learn, as I have, that top performers in sports and business are men and women who've made the choice to become champions and then acted on that choice. They assume total responsibility for their performance, good or bad, and they are willing to do what it takes to succeed.

You will also learn, as I have, that success doesn't care who you are or where you come from. Individuals of all economic backgrounds, ethnicities, genders, shapes, and sizes have made it to the top. Becoming a top performer in your field is not determined by any of those things. It is within *your* control.

Through my consulting work in both sports and business, it's become clear to me that these two worlds have much in common. Both attract competitive, high-achieving individuals who enjoy performing in an environment where winning matters. Both worlds reward individuals and teams that rise to the top, and weed out those who simply don't make the grade. Both worlds include success and failure, peaks and slumps, and winners and losers.

Whether you are competing on the golf course, on the tennis court, to land a new client, win a promotion, or close a major deal, you can become a champion at what you do. Champions are champions because of who they are inside, how they act, and ultimately how they perform. The best in business draw on the same performance essentials as those in the world of sports.

You've probably noticed that this is a short book. And that's deliberate. As I have seen time and time again, champions are determined to identify, focus on, and master the *essentials*—the performance variables that are most important to success in their field of endeavor. They waste no time on things that would, at best, bring them modest gains.

The five key principles outlined in this book will help you master the essentials in whatever you do and provide you with the tools you need to reach ever-higher levels of performance.

Now let's get started.

DRIVE TO THE TOP!

CHAPTER 1

THE CHAMPION INSIDE YOU

TOP PERFORMERS IN GOLF AND OTHER SPORTS ARE NOT GODS, believe me. I've known lots of them and seen more than a few in the locker room. But they differ from many of us mere mortals in two important respects: (1) They have made a *deliberate choice* to be the best at what they do, and (2) they *continuously act* on that choice.

Every top athlete I have ever known has worked tirelessly to control the key factors that influence his or her performance. They assume total responsibility for their results, good or bad, and they are willing to do whatever it takes to improve and keep improving.

The best word to define this special class of athletes and people in other fields, who truly excel at what they do, is "champions." The champions among us have the rare ability to keep their focus on what's important—and to divert their attention from what is not. They understand the essential requirements for becoming the best in the world at what they do. A champion's unwavering determination to master these essentials is, more than anything else, what separates him or her from the rest of the pack.

"The one strongest, most important idea in my game of golf—my cornerstone—is that I want to be the best," Jack Nicklaus, a golfer many would argue is the best of all time, once said. "I wouldn't accept anything less than that. My ability to concentrate and work toward that goal has been my greatest asset."

KNOW WHERE YOU WANT TO GO

One reason many people never seem to accomplish as much as they could in life is that they haven't clearly defined their long-term (or even short-term) destinations. To get the most from the principles in this book, you'll first need to define a destination for yourself.

The destination you choose could be a long-term goal, such as financial independence, early retirement, or the CEO's perch at your company. Or it might be a short-term milestone that gets you that much closer to your long-term goal, such as moving up a notch in the corporate hierarchy, taking charge of a department or division, or landing a large but elusive account you've had your eye on.

While I'm a big believer in setting ambitious, long-term goals, I'm an even bigger believer in maintaining some flexibility. As you move up life's ladder you may well see new rungs (or even entirely new ladders) that you never noticed before.

In fact, rather than that well-worn ladder, I like to use the analogy of a Slinky, you know, the kind you had as a kid. And if you have kids of your own they probably have one too. It's one of the great, all-time classic toys—a champion in its own right. Just in case you've never seen a Slinky, here's a picture of one.

Now let's suppose this Slinky is your career. Imagine it stretched out vertically, with each of its rungs representing a particular milestone on the journey toward your ultimate goal. Think of that lifelong journey as working your way along your Slinky.

As with the rungs on that Slinky, we may sometimes feel we are simply going round and round, unaware that we are actually making progress, though perhaps more slowly than we'd like. Other times, when things are going especially well, we can shoot ahead a rung or two. Now and then something unfortunate happens and we're knocked back a couple of rungs.

I have seen this sort of career path again and again with champion golfers and other athletes. What's different about them is that they simply never stop. Once a champion reaches a particular milestone (or rung on the Slinky), what does he or she do? They set a new and even more challenging goal - and keep moving toward it. Champions are masters at defining the next goal in their plan to be No. 1. They either achieve that next rung of the Slinky, or they retire trying.

Consider one of the great golfers of our (or any other) time, Tiger Woods. As a child, Woods had Jack Nicklaus' career records taped to his bedroom wall and had memorized them. Why? Because beating those records was his ultimate goal. Of course on the way, the young Woods had a few other milestones to visit. Some of the major rungs of his Slinky would look something like this:

- U.S. Junior Amateur Champion, 1991
- U.S. Amateur Champion, 1994
- First PGA Tour win, 1996
- First green jacket at Augusta National, 1997
- PGA Championship, 1999
- U.S. Open and British Open, 2000

Photo by John Iacono, *Sports Illustrated*

"The one strongest, most important idea in my game of golf—my cornerstone— is that I want to be the best." —*Jack Nicklaus*

In other words, Tiger Woods didn't come out of nowhere to become the undisputed top golfer in the world. Though his career is exemplary by any measure, he had to do it rung-by-rung, just like the rest of us. And he's suffered some setbacks too, including a much-publicized slump in 1998.

Maybe you're wondering if this means that to be a champion you can never be happy with what you've achieved or where you are at any given point; absolutely not. Champions also know as well as anybody—and a lot better than most, how to celebrate their successes along the way.

But they don't let themselves reach a plateau and stay there. They refuse to stagnate. As much joy as they take in each and every success, they seem to derive even more pleasure from striving to reach the next goal they've set for themselves.

WHAT MAKES A CHAMPION?

Champions in the worlds of sports and business recognize that the driving force behind any individual's success lies within— inside the heart and soul of the individual. I like to think of that as "character."

Character, as I define it, isn't something that you or I are born with. It develops over time and is influenced both by our experiences in life and the people around us: our parents, our teachers, our bosses, our colleagues, our children, and our friends.

As I've observed many times in my work with top performers, most of them share a particular set of character traits that they constantly draw on while reaching for new levels of success. Many other people have these traits too, but haven't developed them to the same degree that top performers have.

These are the five key traits that seem to set top performers apart. I have yet to meet a top athlete who didn't exemplify them.

1.   Motivation to be the best
2.   The will to work
3.   Total self-discipline
4.   Trust in others
5.   Calculated risk-taking

Let's look at these all-important traits one at a time.

Motivation to Be the Best

The people I call champions want to be the best at what they do—and they're rarely shy about saying so. Unfortunately, the dream of becoming No. 1 in the world at anything is not necessarily encouraged or supported in many educational institutions, workplaces, or even families. Men and women who are willing to dream and strive for their most desired ambitions often must deal with pessimists who challenge them with statements such as, "That would be great, but now let's get back to reality," or "You've got to be dreaming!"

Sometimes the skeptics have a point, oddly enough. Champions do know how to dream, and that is one of the reasons they are champions. Not only do they dream, they dream big. For years, LPGA superstar, Annika Sorenstam, has developed her game and mindset under the guidance of Pia Nilsson, who first coached her when she was a teenager on the Swedish national golf team. In 1989, Nilsson introduced Sorenstam to a concept called Vision54. It represented an ideal of excellence in which a player would strive toward the goal of making a birdie on every hole, thus shooting 54 for an 18-hole round. As Sorenstam later recalled it, "The idea that I could birdie every hole on any golf course in the same round (because at one time or another I had birdied every hole on my home course) truly motivated me." While most golfers use 72 (par) as their benchmark score, Nilsson coached Sorenstam and the other members of the Swedish national team to set a different standard, 54—or 18 shots lower.

Was that dreaming? Unrealistic? I don't think so.

In 2001, Sorenstam moved one step closer to her Vision54 goal when she posted a 59 during the second round of the Standard Register Ping Tournament.

CONTESTANT Annika Sorenstam										OFFICIAL LPGA SCORE CARD									PREVIOUS TOTAL 65 THIS ROUND 59 NEW TOTAL 124	
DATE ___ TEE ___	ID 396 DATE 3/16/01 TEE 10 TIME 8:40 AM PREVIOUS TOTAL: 65																				
HOLES	1	2	3	4	5	6	7	8	9	OUT	10	11	12	13	14	15	16	17	18	IN	TOTAL
YARDS	349	169	336	511	136	393	401	476	363	3154	534	157	394	506	355	177	414	360	408	3305	6459
PAR	4	3	4	5	3	4	4	5	4	36	5	3	4	5	4	3	4	4	4	36	72
	3	2	3	4	3	4	4	4	4	31	4	2	3	4	3	2	3	3	4	28	59

CONTESTANT SIGNATURE   MARKER'S SIGNATURE

Courtesy of the LPGA

Yes, top performers like Sorenstam know how to dream, and once in a while, they wake up to find that they are living the dream!

Champions enjoy competition, and they hate losing. They are willing to break through whatever personal or institutional barriers stand in their way. They believe in themselves and their ability to accomplish whatever they set their minds to. They take control of their destiny and don't depend on others to provide them with the opportunity for success. They create that opportunity themselves.

Champions strive to win whether others support them or not. The possibility of failure rarely enters their mind. Or if it does, they are quick to usher it to the nearest exit. "Confidence is everything," golf great Craig Stadler once said. "From there it's a small step to winning."

The Will to Work

One of the most striking characteristics of the world's best athletes is their willingness to put in whatever amount of work is required to achieve their desired goal. That holds true even after they have filled their trophy cases and have enough prize money to never work again, if they so choose. They are simply driven to outwork other people.

You've heard the phrase, "it's not the quantity, but the quality" of practice that makes a champion. Well, the reality is that it is both the quality *and* the quantity. Arnold Palmer was known for hitting balls eight to 12 hours each day in his prime, and today Vijay Singh can be found practicing from sunup to sundown. There are no shortcuts on the road to becoming a champion or, for that matter, to remaining one.

Several years ago, a veteran PGA Tour player contacted me for help with his game. This individual had a reputation (and stats to support it) for being a phenomenal ball-striker, but a less than average short-game player. He came to see me with the specific intent of identifying the cause of his short-game deficits, and more importantly, to create a training plan and practice strategies that would turn things around. As you might expect, we spent most of the day addressing his short-game skills. Nearing the end of the day, he turned to me and said, "Since we still have some time left in the day, I'd like to know what you think about my long-game practice routines."

> THE DRIVING FORCE BEHIND ANY INDIVIDUAL'S SUCCESS IS CHARACTER.

I quickly responded, "I think they are fantastic."

He replied "But you haven't even seen them! Don't you want me to show you what I do?"

I explained, "Whatever you are doing is working, and working quite well at that. Your ball-striking statistics are nothing less than exceptional, so whatever you are doing, keep doing it! Believe me,

I'll learn a lot more from you than you will from me in this area. Your results speak for themselves."

Nevertheless, as with many great athletes driving for perfection, he still insisted that I take a look at his long-game practice routines. So we headed to the back of the range with his clubs and a teaching basket of balls. As we stepped onto the practice tee, I said, "Okay, show me what you typically do while working on your long-game."

"Do you want me to tell you what I am doing or just show you?" he asked.

"Go about things as if I weren't here," I replied.

He smiled, walked over to his golf bag and pulled out a steel shaft—no grip, no club on the end—just a shaft. He looked over at me with the shaft in one hand and a can of Diet Coke in the other. Then he turned, faced the other end of the driving range and began pacing down the side of the range, counting his paces to himself as he walked. I watched as he walked approximately 125 yards into the driving range, hoping privately that he wouldn't get hit by the stray balls of the novice golfers striving simply to get their balls airborne. When he stopped, he stabbed the shaft vertically into the turf, chugged the remainder of his Diet Coke, and then screwed the can onto the top of the fixed shaft.

He walked back to me at the practice tee, grasped the teaching basket and poured the balls (more than 300) into a large pile on the tee. Then he took his pitching wedge and methodically began hitting balls at the Diet Coke can in the same manner as an archer would fire arrows at the bulls-eye on a target.

I watched as ball after ball increasingly threatened the can's perch on the shaft. Finally, I asked, "Do you actually think that you are going to hit that can with one of those balls?" He confidently replied, "I don't *think* I will, I *know* I will! It's just a matter of how many balls I will have to hit before I do." At that moment, I learned from him what the "will to work" really meant at a world-class level.

In business, the will to work is also essential. The more we work, the more we experience. The more we experience, the more we learn, and the easier things become. Champions recognize that hard work is a key ingredient in their performance formula, and without hard work, successful performance would not come easily.

"The harder I practice," golf legend Gary Player once quipped, "the luckier I get."

Total Self-Discipline

Self-discipline sounds like an old-fashioned virtue, the kind of thing Horatio Alger might have recommended. However, it is anything but old-fashioned to today's top-performing athletes. Their self-discipline is evident in the food they eat, in their sleeping habits, in their training regimens, in their everyday decision-making, and in their time management.

Behavior that to many people seems obsessive, methodical, and monotonous is normal to a top golf pro. Pros have a purpose, and a very detailed one at that, for everything they do during their training. They do not simply "beat balls" and play golf with no intent. Because they have very little free time, touring pros demand that their instruction time, workouts, and practice periods be of the highest quality. Rigorous time-management becomes essential.

Champions focus their attention on a well-defined goal, and they have the self-discipline to prioritize their life and activities around the choices that will have the greatest impact on achieving their goal. LPGA Champion Beth Daniel once told me, "I'm disciplined when it comes to golf. I'm terrible at paperwork. If it's something that I'm interested in, I'm disciplined almost to a fault. Furman [where Daniel studied] was a liberal-arts college, and we had to take

Photo by Fred Vuich, *Sports Illustrated*

"The harder I practice, the luckier I get." —*Gary Player*

Language and Religion—those were required courses and I wasn't interested, and I didn't make very good grades in them. But then, I made A's in Kinesiology, Anatomy, Exercise Physiology—I aced all of those courses. I was interested in them so I really applied myself and was very disciplined in those classes."

Often, discipline involves some personal sacrifices (which could even translate into below-average performance in some coursework) in order to laser-focus your attention on the factors that most contribute to the achievement of your goals.

Self-discipline has its own rewards, however, and one of them is that it provides an athlete with a powerful sense of personal accomplishment. To the athlete, "accomplishment" doesn't necessarily mean winning, even though winning is almost certainly their intended outcome. Instead, athletes experience accomplishment through the completion of their daily plan—a plan that has been designed to give them the greatest possible opportunity for success.

As I have seen many times in my work, the satisfaction experienced by a player who has created a plan and exhibits the self-discipline to stick to that plan is phenomenal. And so are the results when the time comes to perform. For example, in 2002, Tiger Woods split from his long-time coach/mentor Butch Harmon. Shortly thereafter he began working with Dallas-based instructor Hank Haney to see if he could take his game to an even higher level. The adage, "You may have to get worse before you get better" was never truer. Woods regressed from the complete dominance he had achieved in 2000, when he led almost every major statistical category in golf and had won more than nine million dollars.

By 2004, however, he had dropped from No. 1 to No. 3 on the PGA Tour money list. Serious as that may have seemed, his ball-striking stats suggested an even more significant slump, with his greens-in-regulation ranking dropping from No. 1 to No. 40, and his driving stats ranking from No. 1 to No. 71.

So what did Tiger Woods do in the face of this declining performance? He stuck to his plan. He had faith in the plan that he and Hank Haney had set, and he believed that with time, effort, and lots of practice, he would reap the rewards. Woods' behavior was very different from that of the typical novice golfer, who takes a lesson or two from a pro, fails to see immediate results, and then goes looking for another pro.

The great Arnold Palmer once told me that his father had taught him one of the most valuable lessons he had learned in life, "Stick to something long enough to master it." Doing just that, Palmer said, was a primary factor in his success.

Self-discipline is also vital in business, of course. A moment ago I was talking about the importance of both quality and quantity of practice to the golfer. In business, quality is closely tied to self-discipline. The real measure of your self-discipline is how efficiently you use your time, your energy, and all your other resources in pursuit of your goals.

Trust in Others

Champions are smart enough to know when they need help, and they are not embarrassed to ask for it. World-class athletes turn to coaches, athletic trainers, sports psychologists, biomechanists, physical therapists, and sports optometrists for the assistance they need to stay on track.

After winning his second U.S. Open in 2004, Retief Goosen was asked how sports psychologist Jos Vanstiphout had helped him prepare for his earlier victory. "I always felt my swing was pretty much there," Goosen explained, "but I knew on the inside I wasn't thinking right. I wasn't positive enough, not focusing enough on

Photo by John G. Zimmerman, *Sports Illustrated*

"Stick to something long enough to master it." —*Arnold Palmer*

what's in hand and thinking of too many other things going on around the course. That's when I started working with Jos."

Jack Nicklaus has spoken many times of the debt he owes to his longtime teacher, Jack Grout. Nicklaus told me that he started working with Grout when he was only ten, and that relationship continued through most of Nicklaus's career as a PGA Tour player. In other words, even after Jack Nicklaus had become one of the most successful athletes in the history of the game, he still needed his teacher's advice.

Part of the reason was because Grout was able to help Nicklaus understand the "whys" of a particular situation. If Nicklaus was in a slump, he knew that he was in a slump. That wasn't the problem. What he didn't know was *why* he was in a slump. But once he did know, with Grout's help, he could start to do something about it. By the same token, if he was performing well, Nicklaus wanted to understand *why* he was performing well. Jack Grout was able to bring that kind of perspective to the situation that Nicklaus couldn't do by himself.

Another great golfer, Phil Mickelson, offered this high praise for his longtime caddy, Jim "Bones" McKay, in a 2005 interview: "He's been very helpful in a lot of areas, but he is very clutch and comes through at critical times with pulling the right clubs or reading the right breaks on the greens, and I'm very fortunate to have him. He's saved me a lot of shots and has been instrumental in a number of my wins, if not all of them."

Effective businesspeople do much the same thing. They know how to draw on the best expertise from all levels of their organizations. And when necessary, they reach outside of their organization for expertise it doesn't possess.

Over the years I've trained thousands of financial advisors, working for such prestigious firms as Merrill Lynch, Morgan

Stanley, and Smith Barney. In years past, such advisors often spent much of their time researching companies and managing stock portfolios for individual clients. Today, however, advisors are able to call on professional money managers from both within and outside their firms, to handle those tasks. That allows the advisors to focus on more essential tasks, such as maintaining client relationships and helping them (clients) with their long-term financial plans.

Top performers know that their efforts multiply exponentially as they learn to rely on others. Winners are able to let go of control where their control isn't absolutely essential, to empower others, to delegate tasks and responsibility, and to thrive on the accomplishments and efforts of those around them. In business, as in sports, champions must build effective teams that collectively work toward a common goal. Individuals who are unable to let go of any control, who feel compelled to micromanage every last detail, or do not have the ability to empower and trust others to succeed, as well, will never reach as high a level.

Calculated Risk-Taking

Great athletes, like great entrepreneurs, are risk-takers. They're willing to accept the risks that go with the game. Of course, in return, they want a fair shot at the rewards. However, they aren't crazy. They don't take just any risks. They take calculated risks. And the difference couldn't be more important.

Great athletes, again like successful businesspeople, protect themselves against the risks they face, by rigorous preparation and planning. They become masters at planning as well as execution. Many top golfers, for example, swear by the practice of visualization. They picture themselves driving the ball straight down the fairway or sinking that long putt from the fringe of the green. Then they step up and, if all goes well, execute the shot exactly as they imagined it.

Most of us make plans, of course. Corporations have entire departments devoted to the practice. But here's where top performers in both sports and business differ from their less-successful peers. Once they have committed to a plan, they put it into action immediately. No hemming, no hawing. No meetings, no committees (or

> # CHAMPIONS
> ## WALK THE TALK.

no more than absolutely necessary). They take the initiative to get things done, and they accept the risks. They don't procrastinate, and they don't look back. In short, champions "walk the talk."

In sports, game day forces players and coaches to execute their plans. There is no more time for delay or re-evaluation. Game day means it's time to take that calculated risk, to see if your strategy, your plans, your ideas will work when it counts. Game day is the time to take action—win or lose.

Professional golfers understand that they put their game plan and skills to the test each time they tee it up. If they don't perform to their liking, they take action once again—heading directly to the practice tee or putting green to further develop their skills.

Professional salespeople, perhaps more than anyone else in business, can relate to both the pressure and exhilaration the athlete experiences on game day. Every sales call can be a "game day" in its own right.

In much of the business world, however, procrastination often seems closer to the norm. Risks aren't just calculated but recalculated, analyzed and then reanalyzed. Meanwhile opportunity may have moved on, taking the potential rewards along with it.

Top performers, however, don't let that happen. They understand, as well as their athlete counterparts, that without timely and effective execution, even the best plans are meaningless. For them, planning isn't a goal, but simply a means to a goal. They know that there is a time to stop planning and start doing.

In their book, *Execution: The Discipline of Getting Things Done,* former Honeywell International Chairman Larry Bossidy and business consultant Ram Charan highlighted the need to move beyond strategy, and execute. They contend that, "When companies fail to deliver on their promises, the most frequent explanation is that the CEO's strategy was wrong. But the strategy by itself is not often the cause. Strategies most often fail because they aren't executed well. Things that are supposed to happen don't happen."

So ask yourself, how effective are you at moving beyond analysis, planning, and strategy and taking a leap of faith to put your ideas to the test. There comes a time when all champions must take a calculated risk if they're going to make things happen.

DO YOU DEMONSTRATE THE CHARACTER OF A CHAMPION?

Now that we've talked a bit about top performers and what's required to become one, I'd like you to take a few minutes to do this short self-assessment exercise. Be brutally honest. Write your answers in the book or on a separate sheet of paper. No one ever has to see them but you.

This exercise should help you see where you stand and what you might want to begin to work on. After completing the assessment, you'll have room to jot down your own personal action plan.

Read the following statements and consider how true each one is of you. Place an "S" by those that are very descriptive of you and an "L" by those that don't describe you very well.

_____ 1. In my profession, I strive to be the best.

_____ 2. I enjoy working and have a strong work ethic.

_____ 3. I rarely get sidetracked from what I plan to do each day.

_____ 4. I am comfortable delegating tasks and responsibilities to others.

_____ 5. Although failure is possible, I take calculated risks to get ahead.

_____ 6. I believe that I ultimately control my own success.

_____ 7. I believe that good things come to those who put in the work.

_____ 8. I avoid and say "no" to activities and tasks that are of low priority.

_____ 9. I surround myself with others who help me obtain my goals.

_____ 10. I don't simply talk about what I want to do, I take action. I "walk the talk."

As you may have noticed, these 10 statements are all related to the five key traits of champions I discussed: motivation to be the best (1 and 6), the will to work (2 and 7), total self-discipline (3 and 8), trust in others (4 and 9), and calculated risk-taking (5 and 10). Your "S" answers above indicate personal characteristics that will *support* you in your effort to be a top performer, while any "L" answers indicate those that currently *limit* you and that you'll want to work on with the help of this book.

CREATE AN ACTION PLAN

Now, as you answer the following questions, consider the statements above that you marked as being limitations for you as well as any other insights you've had as you've read this chapter.

These questions are designed to help you identify actions that you can take to further develop your inner champion.

1. *Of the five key character traits described in this chapter— motivation to be the best, the will to work, total self-discipline, trust in others, and calculated risk-taking—are there any you feel could be holding you back in achieving your goals? If so, what are they?*

_____

_____

_____

2. *If you listed any weak areas above, why do you think that you have yet to sufficiently develop them? (For example, you may not feel passionate about your work or you are not sure of the specific steps you should take, or where to begin, to develop such character traits.)*

_____

_____

_____

3. *Name one or more people you know and have access to who demonstrate the character trait(s) in which you are weak.*

_____

_____

_____

4. *How do they demonstrate such character trait(s)? Try to think of specific behaviors that you could replicate.*

_____

_____

_____

5. *What specific actions can you take to improve in those areas? (For example, you might consider hiring a coach, taking a course, pursuing a mentor, reading a relevant book a month, and/or surrounding yourself with appropriate role models.) List one to three specific actions that you will take. And to make this real, give yourself a deadline for each of them.*

Action #1:

_____

_____

_____

Completion Date: _____

Action #2:

_____

_____

_____

Completion Date: _____

Action #3:

_____

_____

_____

Completion Date: _____

BRING OUT THE CHAMPION IN YOU

In my work, I have been privileged to see many top golfers and other athletes push themselves. I've seen them reach limits that even they thought were beyond them. I believe that most of us, athletes or not, have far more potential than we know.

Tapping that potential is a never-ending process—a journey that you commit to every day as you strive to move up those rungs of the

Slinky. This process can be broken into five essential steps. I'll briefly discuss each of them now and in more detail later. As you read and think about them, bear in mind that these five essentials are interdependent; each one relies on the other four if you're to achieve real results. Your long-term success will be directly related to your ability to master all five.

Those five essential steps are:

1.   Define Your Goal
2.   Know What It Takes
3.   Measure Where You Stand
4.   Train Like a Champion
5.   Take It to the Course

Essential Step #1: Define Your Goal

The first essential to taking your game to the next level is to focus on one or several specific goals. Make them things you feel passionate about and truly desire. As Jack Nicklaus once observed, "I'm a firm believer that people only do their best at things they truly enjoy. It is difficult to excel at something you don't enjoy."

Champions in all walks of life are passionate about what they do. Their core beliefs, attitudes, daily routines, personal motivation, and work ethic all appear to be directed toward one ambition; becoming the best. That kind of intense focus is key to taking your performance to a world-class level.

Donald J. Trump, the real estate tycoon and promoter extraordinaire, put it this way not long ago on The Trump Blog, "I'm a firm believer that passion is absolutely necessary in order to achieve comprehensive success. I say 'comprehensive' because in order to be truly successful, it's important that you feel fulfilled by what you're doing. Otherwise, what's the point? Empty success is success without passion. It's like going to school and tuning in just enough to pass,

TO BE A CHAMPION, BE YOURSELF

While I believe that champions in all walks of life share certain essential characteristics, I have noticed something else about them; in many other ways, they couldn't be more different.

True champions are as individual as snowflakes, fingerprints, or, for that matter, golf swings.

Consider, for example, Jim Furyk, the 2003 U.S. Open winner. Furyk's loopy backswing, built under the guidance of his coach and father, Mike, has become his trademark. Referring to Furyk's swing, the sportswriter Jim Murray said he'd, "seen more form on a guy fighting a swarm of bees." Furyk responded, "It's been called worse. But it works for me."

Jim Furyk understands one of golf's most important, yet least understood principles; controlling the ball is essential, but looking good while you're doing it is not. Lee Trevino, another famously idiosyncratic ball striker, once remarked that his swing consisted of "five wrongs to make a right at impact…the only bit that matters."

Champions in golf master what's essential, control over appearance, function over form, and results over style.

So, too, do the top performers in business. If they are unable to deliver the goods, they are not likely to remain on top very long. Business is a game of results. And it rewards men and women who know and trust their ability to deliver those results rather than waste time trying to be someone they're not.

Becoming a champion isn't about being someone else. It's about drawing on resources that have been inside you all along.

Photo by John Biever, *Sports Illustrated*

"When I'm playing well I can repeat that swing and that's why I think it has held up and that's why it has worked under pressure." —*Jim Furyk*

so that you can get out and do what you really *want* to be doing...."
Perhaps not surprisingly, the relentlessly competitive Trump is also
a passionate golfer.

Essential Step #2: Know What It Takes

While the desire to succeed is essential, so is the knowledge of
what it takes to get there. Imagine having the drive, determination,
and discipline of an Annika Sorenstam, but lacking the knowledge
of what you need to do when you get to the practice range.
Champions like Sorenstam and Tiger Woods obviously know what
it takes to succeed in golf. They know what skills are needed to get
to the top and they know what it takes to develop those skills.

Champions in the business world are also able to identify the
critical skills required to get ahead in their organizations and
industries. As a teenager, Michael Dell, later to become founder and
CEO of Dell Computer, was tearing apart Apple II computers to
see how they worked. After his freshman year at the University of
Texas, Dell dropped out to start his own company. "I was in college
for a year, so I got to experience many of the things people go to
college for," Dell subsequently explained. "The objective of going
to college is to learn—and I think I've learned more doing what I've
been doing than I ever could have in college."

Michael Dell recognized early on that college wasn't providing
him with the critical skills he needed to become a pioneer in the rapidly
evolving personal computer industry. Top performers have almost a
sixth sense about locating the knowledge they need to achieve their
dreams, and if the traditional paths like college don't provide it, they
quickly switch to other avenues. Microsoft's Bill Gates is another
celebrated college dropout, in his case, from Harvard.

I'm certainly not suggesting that any college students reading
this book should walk off campus tomorrow. Without college, I

never would have been able to attain my own goals in life. The point is that, depending on what you want to accomplish, you may have to look beyond the traditional knowledge centers to find what you're looking for. Risky as it may sometimes seem, champions in sports, business, or whatever, take their search for knowledge in their own hands, and they take it very seriously indeed.

Essential Step #3: Measure Where You Stand

You've probably heard the phrase, "If you don't know where you're going, any road will take you there." More important for our purposes, consider that, "If you don't know where you are, how do you know which way to go?" Champions make sure they know where they stand, relative to their own accomplishments, relative to their competitors, and relative to the goals that they have set for the future. They may not always like the answers, but they know they have to have them in order to decide how to spend their working time.

Measuring where you stand means having a system in place so you can constantly evaluate your performance against what's needed to succeed in your line of work. Most PGA Tour players, for example, know where they stand in comparison to the top ten players on specific statistical measures.

In business, this is referred to as "benchmarking." Men or women at the top of a company or an industry set the benchmark, the standard, by which others can measure where they stand.

How do you compare with the best in your business? In the results-oriented world of sales, for example, professional salespeople are constantly measuring themselves against the higher-producing performers in their company. If someone is producing twice the sales volume per year, the others want to know why. Simply knowing the outcome is not enough. They want to know what is driving that outcome. Is it the number of prospects the star seller sees each day, the close ratio per opportunity, the average dollar value of a sale, the number of referrals from previous clients…or what?

Identifying the causes of the performance gaps between the star performer and everyone else allows others to begin to close those gaps.

Essential Step #4: Train Like a Champion

Measuring where you stand in comparison to the best in your line of work does not lead to success all by itself, of course. Once you've identified your performance gaps you must then begin to address them, systematically and wholeheartedly. That's what I mean by "train like a champion."

Professional athletes know that their performance on game day is directly related to the quality of their training. World-class golfers have learned to effectively use the driving range, the practice green, and the golf course to improve their swing, fine-tune their short-game skills, and cut strokes off their scores.

In business, you must also train like a champion to build the essential skills required to take your performance to the next level. That means never resting on your past accomplishments, but continuously pressing ahead to collect new ones.

As Dwight D. Eisenhower, World War II commander, U.S. President, and passionate amateur golfer, once observed, "Neither a wise man nor a brave man lies down on the tracks of history to wait for the train of the future to run over him."

Consider, for example, the strategy of corporate giant Microsoft. Rather than wait for a competitor to come along and make its products obsolete, it does that itself, regularly updating its Windows platform—Windows 1.0, Windows 95, Windows 98, Windows ME, Windows XP, and Windows Vista—in order to stay

THE REWARDS OF DISCIPLINE

By far, the most striking characteristic that stands out among all of the world's best athletes is discipline. For many people, "discipline" has a negative connotation. They feel constrained by the boundaries involved in living a disciplined life.

Great golfers, on the other hand, thrive on the discipline that they "choose" to guide their day-to-day choices. They engage in disciplined routines each and every day that directly contribute to their intended results. Here are a few concrete examples of discipline that I see in the champions I work with:

- Hitting 100 putts in-a-row from four feet every day
- Working out from six to eight a.m. five days a week
- Stretching for 15 minutes before every practice session and round of golf
- Warming up for one hour before every competitive round
- Practicing for two hours in 90 degree heat—after finishing a five-hour tournament round
- Flying across the country to train with their instructor for one to two days every other month
- Hitting 600 to 800 balls per day, while focusing on a few key aspects of their swing

Sounds exhausting, doesn't it? It is, but it's worth it! The sense of personal accomplishment is what it's all about. The self-fulfillment experienced by a player who has set high goals and followed a disciplined program to reach those goals is fantastic.

What behaviors do you execute on a regular basis that demonstrates your discipline? Are you around others who exemplify discipline, or do your peers epitomize laziness? Discipline does not have to be something imposed on you by someone else. Champions impose it on themselves.

a step (or more) ahead of its constantly evolving, performance-driven competitors.

When entrepreneur Reed Hastings launched a business renting DVDs by mail in 1998, he knew that the technology to download movies off the Internet would eventually make his service obsolete. So rather than put DVD in the name of his new company, he called it NetFlix, positioning it to ride that next wave as well.

Essential Step #5: Take It to the Course

Superbly hitting the ball on the driving range is one thing. Transferring that skill to the course is another matter entirely. One of the most common questions asked by amateur golfers of sport psychologists is, "Why can I hit it so well on the driving range during a lesson with my pro, but when I'm competing in a friendly Nassau with my foursome on the weekend, I revert right back to my old ways?"

The answer is that many golfers, pros included, take months to become comfortable using a new skill, especially in competition. But the longer it takes to transfer that skill to the course, the longer they have to wait to reap the rewards. That's why professional golfers develop mental toughness skills, practice regimens, and performance strategies to ensure that they can take their game to the course, where it really counts.

Business professionals must develop similar strategies and skills to succeed under the competitive pressure and demands placed on them every day. Whether it's closing a crucial deal, making a pitch for a promotion, or any other high-stakes opportunity, they also have to perform under pressure.

Do you have the ability to take it to the course and perform to your potential when the opportunity arises? I'll provide more information about that and the other essential steps in later chapters of this book.

PUTTING IT ALL TOGETHER

This diagram shows how all five essential steps fit together.

Notice that they don't form a straight line, but a circle. That's because the process never ends, at least for those who are determined to become top performers. Once you have successfully completed one cycle, you'll go on to the next one, just like moving up the rungs of the Slinky.

Each time you strive to advance your career to the next level, you should update your goals, examine what it will take to get there, measure yourself against established benchmarks, refine your training, and then take it to the course. Becoming a champion is all about applying these five essentials to your unique situation.

CHAPTER 2

DEFINE YOUR GOAL

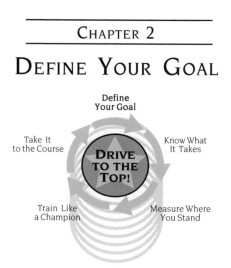

BEFORE WE BEGIN THIS CHAPTER, PLEASE READ THE STATEMENTS BELOW and consider how descriptive each one is of you. Using a one-to-five scale (five being very descriptive, and one being not very descriptive) rate each item as it applies to you.

_____ 1.   I am clear about what I want to do with my career.

_____ 2.   My current career path (or academic path) is in an area in which I am extremely interested.

_____ 3.   I value the work that I do very much, because it fulfills exactly what I want from a job.

_____ 4.   I have the necessary skills to succeed in my desired career.

_____ 5.   My goals are *my* goals, not someone else's.

_____ 6.   I know what my vocational interests are, and I can define specific jobs that are in alignment with my interests.

_____ 7.   To maximize my job satisfaction, I know exactly what I want and need in a job.

_____ 8.   I know the skills required to be successful in my career.

Take note of the items on the previous page that you ranked with a three or less. As you read on, consider how you might focus on those areas to better define your goals.

When you saw the title of this chapter, *Define Your Goal*, I bet the word that seemed to be most significant was "Goal." We've all heard experts say that you have to set goals, reach for goals, achieve goals, and measure goals. Yes, goals are important, but even more important is that *you* define *your* goal! In other words, you should be striving for something that *you* defined, that *you* want, and that *you* are passionate about!

It seems pretty obvious that Tiger Woods has a goal—to be the best golfer in the world, possibly the best ever to play the game. Having such a goal is important for Woods, but exponentially more important is that the goal is *his*. Because of the attention given to his father, Earl Woods, many fans mistakenly assumed that Tiger's goals were defined by his dad. Earl Woods ran the risk of getting lumped in with all of those overbearing parents who seem to be living their lives through the successes of their children. However, Tiger Woods' situation is different. His goals are *his*, not his father's. As he said prior to his father passing away, "Don't force your kids into sports. I never was. To this day, my dad has never asked me to go play golf; I ask him. It's the child's desire to play that matters, not the parent's desire to have the child play. Fun. Keep it fun."

Tiger's love for the game, pursuit of perfection, and thirst for competition came from within. That's what matters! An intrinsic motivation to succeed, regardless of what the goal is, is the fuel that drives most champions' accomplishments.

Before most of us had ever heard of Tiger Woods, Michael Jordan was the Tiger Woods of sports. At the core of Jordan's success was his love for the game. "I didn't really get instruction until I was a junior in high school," he once recalled. "First, I just

Photo by V. J. Lovero, *Sports Illustrated*

"It's the child's desire to play that matters,
not the parent's desire to have the child play. Fun. Keep it fun." —*Tiger Woods*

loved the game, and I let my skills develop. So I believe in learning late—playing early, but learning late." Jordan had plenty of time to develop his skills, receive coaching, practice, and compete. His first step on the road to success was learning to enjoy the game.

The great Pittsburgh Steelers quarterback and Pro Football Hall of Fame inductee Terry Bradshaw has spent his life living his passion—football. As a college and pro player, and more recently as a TV commentator, he demonstrated an undeniable devotion to the sport. As Bradshaw once reflected, "If God would come down right now [and ask me], 'Terry, what can I do for you?' [I'd say] 'Send me in, put me back in one Super Bowl, and put me on the one-foot line, and give me two minutes to go, and all three of my timeouts and give me my boys.'"

Yes, professional athletes like Tiger Woods, Michael Jordan, and Terry Bradshaw have it good; they get to play a game they love, and get paid handsomely for it. But keep in mind that this enviable connection between passion and career was not just handed to them. No matter how athletically gifted they may have been to begin with, they earned their shot at the pros via hard work, discipline, sacrifice, and an unyielding commitment to their dream. Before they were legends, they were normal people struggling to find their place in this world, just like the rest of us.

Speaking of the rest of us; when I was still an undergraduate in college I used to teach golf in the summer at Chase Golf and Tennis Camps in Bethlehem, New Hampshire. I had no aspirations of teaching golf for a living. It was simply a summer job, but I found that I loved it. I loved the process of coaching, teaching, and helping others succeed. I also liked being outdoors, visiting different golf courses, working with different people from various countries, and learning from those I taught. The job paid next to nothing, but I didn't care. I was young, carefree, had few expenses to worry about, and hey, it was just a summer job. Summers were a time to enjoy life and rest up for the work to come once I returned to school.

One spring semester, a good friend asked me, "What are you going to do when you graduate?"

I responded, "Go to dental school and become a dentist."

"So you want to have your fingers in people's mouths all day?" he asked.

I thought to myself, "No way!" But I also realized I had never really examined the matter carefully. I just was intent on being a doctor of some kind because that seemed like a good ambition, one that I shared with a lot of other guys.

The next day I decided that dental school wasn't really for me. However, I still didn't know what I *did* want to do with my life. Two years later, I graduated with a bachelor's degree in psychology. Since I had no idea what I wanted to do, I had applied to graduate school to study psychology. Why? To get a doctorate, I guess, and also to delay the inevitable—heading out into the world of work with no experience, no goal, and no idea of what I really wanted to do with my life.

While I was in graduate school, I read *Do What You Love, the Money Will Follow* by Marsha Sinetar. It resonated with me like nothing else I'd ever read. Sinetar's book helped me clarify my view of the world of work and how I intended to interact with it. I recognized that work didn't have to be just a necessary evil. It wasn't something you do solely to earn money in order to pay for the things you really love. I realized it was possible to do something that didn't feel like work. The key was doing work that you love.

So, I asked myself, "What do I love?"

And the answer came pretty easily. I loved people, sports, coaching, teaching, being outdoors, travel, and helping others succeed.

If you've never asked yourself that question, now would be a very good time.

Not long after that, a woman I knew happened to tell me, "I saw a man on television today that was so much like you, and he was in a job that would be just perfect for you." I asked her what he did, and she said, "He was a sports psychologist. He coaches professional athletes."

Wow, I thought. A perfect fit. I revised my educational plan, pursued a specialization in exercise science and sports psychology, and have never looked back.

Now I spend my working life doing something that I would frankly do for free (I just don't want my clients to know that!). For the last 15 years, my "office" has been on the golf course at the beautiful PGA National Resort and Spa in Palm Beach Gardens, Florida. I work with world-class athletes who have taught me more about success, character, self-discipline, and achievement than I could've ever learned in academia. My passion is my work; what a deal!

Are you passionate about what you do? Did you, like me, first head down a path toward something that you simply were not passionate about? Have you corrected your mistake? Remember, it's never too late to take control of your life and do what you love.

I'm not saying that you have to stop everything you are doing, quit your job, sell your house, and go spend a year on a mountaintop, soul-searching your way to starvation. Finding and attaining your passion is an ongoing process, a series of decisions, each of which brings you that much closer toward a perfect match between what you really want and what you are actually doing.

In other words, you don't have to make wholesale changes. I worked for a counseling center in college and had the opportunity to consult with the athletic department as one part of my job responsibilities. That gave me some useful experience and brought me a step closer to my ultimate goal of working with athletes as a career. I've known financial advisors who focus their efforts on polo players because they have a passion for the sport and want eventually to work their way into it full-time.

Richard Branson, the British entrepreneur behind Virgin Atlantic Airways and a diverse collection of other business interests, expressed a similar view in an interview with the magazine *Business 2.0* several years ago. Asked how much would-be entrepreneurs should focus on the bottom line, Branson said, "Ideally, since 80 percent of your life is spent working, you should start your business around something that is a passion of yours. If you're into kite-surfing and you want to become an entrepreneur, do it with kite-surfing. Look, if you can indulge in your passion, life will be far more interesting than if you're just working. You'll work harder at it, and you'll know more about it. But first you must go out and educate yourself on whatever it is you've decided to do—know more about kite-surfing than anyone else. But if you're doing things you're passionate about, that will come naturally."

For many of us, now may not seem like the time for even incremental changes. Maybe you're raising a family, paying off debts, caring for a loved one, or busy with some other critical demand. However, never let your life-situation stop you from, at the very least, considering what you might do to take just one step in the journey toward your passion.

My wife is currently a stay-at-home mom, yet she's working more than she ever worked while employed. She has a master's degree in education, taught elementary school for 10 years and, might I say, has an unquenchable thirst for contributing to the education of youth in America. Raising our two children has not prevented her from pursuing her passion. She serves on the Parent Teacher Association, volunteers regularly in the classroom, organizes school-

Photo by Justin Sullivan, *Getty Images*

"If you can indulge in your passion,
life will be far more interesting than if you're just working." —*Sir Richard Branson*

wide functions, and coordinates training programs for teachers' continuing education. She, as I often joke, works more in the school system now than she did when she was employed as a full-time teacher. For her, it's not about being paid, it's about educating children and those involved in this pursuit.

Commitment is all about focusing your attention and taking small, progressive steps in a defined direction. Let's not understate the "defined direction" part of this last statement. Taking steps in twenty different directions is the equivalent of treading water—there's a lot of activity, but you are going nowhere. Before you jump in the water, you have to decide which way you intend to swim.

YOU'RE GOING ON AN EXPLORATION

Defining the direction of your career and life is not an easy task. For many of us, the process is one of trial and error, and it often takes several trials before we stop making errors.

Unfortunately, many people have little exposure during their early years to all the possibilities the world of work offers. As a result they often end up in jobs that fall far short of what they would truly enjoy doing.

Regardless of where you are at this moment in your life, I encourage you to continue your exploration of what it would take to find true passion in your work life, if you don't have it already. You deserve nothing less! Work does not have to feel like work! It's okay to get paid for doing the things you actually

> BEFORE YOU JUMP IN THE WATER, YOU HAVE TO DECIDE WHICH WAY YOU INTEND TO SWIM.

love. As you take incremental steps toward the perfect match between you and your career, there are three factors that you should focus on: (1) your interests, (2) your work values, and (3) your skills. We'll take them one by one.

1. Your Interests

Are you currently engaged in a job that you enjoy? How interested are you in the activities that you do day to day? Have you ever taken the time to explore your career interests and make career choices that are in better alignment with these interests? Your level of career satisfaction can be directly linked to the choices that you have made in your career path over time; choices that are still within your control.

Many of today's tools for assessing people's career choices are based in the work of the psychologist John Holland. He divided career interests into six different vocational personality types: realistic, investigative, artistic, social, enterprising, and conventional.

Holland's theory is that most of us match up with one or several of these six types, and once you've determined where you fit, you'll benefit by finding a work environment that is consistent with it.

For instance, professional athletes are often individuals categorized by Holland as "realistic." That means they're active, straightforward, self-reliant people interested in manual activities that require motor coordination and physical skills. No wonder we often hear athletes saying things like, "I'm living my dream. Who wouldn't enjoy going to the golf course every day and getting paid for it?" Professional athletes have not accidentally ended up in the world of sports; they have actively pursued an area of great interest to them.

LIFE'S TOO SHORT TO SPEND IT COMPLAINING

Do you know people who seem to spend every waking hour griping about all the things that are wrong or difficult in their lives? "My job stinks." "My boss is a micromanager." "My kids are driving me crazy." Insert your favorite complaint here.

As the old saying goes, their glass is half-empty, not half-full. And not only that, it's probably dirty and maybe even cracked. At least that's how they see it.

Where does this attitude come from? Some people, I believe, become pessimistic because they feel trapped doing something they have little intrinsic interest in. Others may have tried to pursue what really interested them in life but suffered setbacks that ruined the experience for them.

People who have been emotionally scarred will go to great lengths to avoid similar experiences in the future—even to the point of forgoing the pursuit of what might really bring them happiness. It's a sad paradox; in their effort to avoid additional pain in their lives, they stop searching for pleasure.

As Dwight D. Eisenhower observed in a characteristically to-the-point statement, "Pessimism never won any battle." You will find few, if any, pessimists in the upper ranks of sports or business. Top performers, whatever the field, understand that failure is an expected, periodic phenomenon associated with the pursuit of excellence.

So if you ever feel the dark cloud of pessimism intruding on your thoughts, ask yourself what are the opportunities, however small they may be, that exist in your present situation. Are you actively pursuing them? And, what else could you start doing today to create greater opportunities for your future?

The Donald Trumps of this world, however, are more "enterprising." They're ambitious, enthusiastic individuals interested in leading, selling, and persuading others as a way to obtain organizational goals or economic gain. Trump himself has reflected on the value of pursuing a career that's consistent with a person's true interests. He's said, "If you're interested in 'balancing' work and pleasure, stop trying to balance them. Instead, make your work more pleasurable."

By focusing on our interests in this way, life becomes an exploration, the search for a better fit between what we are really interested in doing and what we actually do every day. So ask yourself where your true interests are. Are you passionate about what you do and the people you work with each day? How could you adjust your current job situation to move one step closer to doing something that you would love to do?

If you would like to spend some time further exploring your career interests, there are wonderful resources available for you. Here are two of them:

1. Take Dr. Holland's self-directed search ($9.95) at www.self-directed-search.com.
2. Read *What Color is Your Parachute? Workbook: How to Paint a Picture of Your Ideal Job or Next Career*, by Richard Nelson Bolles.

2. Your Work Values

Besides being in line with your interests, research suggests that to be a good fit for you, a job needs to meet your work values. Below is a checklist of common work values that different people seek in their jobs. Take a look at the list and check off the ones that are most important to you in a work situation. Feel free to write in other things you value if they're not already on the list.

Photo by Dave Allocca, *Getty Images*

"Become the change you want to see—those are words I live by." —*Oprah Winfrey*

EXPLORING YOUR WORK VALUES

- ☐ Autonomy
- ☐ Challenge and adventure
- ☐ Control of time
- ☐ Creativity
- ☐ Excitement
- ☐ Expertise
- ☐ Financial wealth
- ☐ Good working conditions
- ☐ Helping others
- ☐ High income
- ☐ Independence
- ☐ Influence
- ☐ Leadership
- ☐ Learning opportunity
- ☐ Power
- ☐ Prestige
- ☐ Recognition
- ☐ Security
- ☐ Stability
- ☐ Variety
- ☐ Other: _____
- ☐ Other: _____

Does your current work situation support the values that you have selected? In the ideal world, what we value and what we do in our jobs would be in perfect alignment. But who lives in the ideal world, right?

The purpose of these self-exploration activities is not to discourage you, nor to remind you that your work life is probably imperfect. Most of ours are, in one way or another. The point is to better understand the factors that contribute to your satisfaction, your passion, and your love for what you spend so many of your working hours doing. As my mother-in-law often says to me, "You get to wake up and do what you love every day! That's not reality for most people. You should feel blessed!" I do, and I hope you do, too.

But if you don't, here's a suggestion. Take a close look at your typical work day—the tasks you complete, the people you interact with, the environment within which you work. What might you do to create a better fit between your work and the work values you checked off above? Stop for a moment to jot down a few ideas— several concrete actions you could take to bring your work values more into your daily life.

Top 3 ranked values:

#1. _____

   Actions to create a better fit:

   _____

   _____

#2. _____

   Actions to create a better fit:

   _____

   _____

#3. _____

   Actions to create a better fit:

   _____

   _____

3. *Your Skills*

To succeed at any job, you need a certain set of skills, whether they're basic or highly specialized. Looking at yourself as honestly as possible, what skills would you say you currently possess? What skills do you need to develop to move your career to the next level? What skills are you currently trying to improve?

In the world of golf, players like Phil Mickelson and Lorena Ochoa are constantly evaluating and improving their skills. To play on tour, they must master the essential golf skills: ball striking, putting, chipping, pitching, etc. As they progress, other skill requirements emerge, such as managing their time, managing their media appearances, and, ultimately, managing their managers (who in turn manage their schedules, their image, their endorsements, and their money).

In your field, whatever it may be, you should also be looking ahead to the skills you'll need once you reach the next level. In the chapter that follows, we'll discuss how you can identify the factors that drive performance in your industry, and several of those are likely to be critical personal skills. You may already have some of those skills. Others you may still need to develop.

So take a moment and consider your skills, both those you have and those you wish you did. These may include interpersonal, managerial, administrative, sales, technical, mechanical, athletic, numerical, service, leadership, artistic, or any other skills you can think of.

My personal skills exploration:

1. I believe that I am most skilled in the areas of:

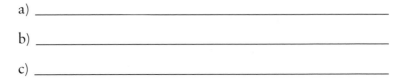

    a) _____

    b) _____

    c) _____

JUST BECAUSE YOU'RE GOOD AT SOMETHING, DOESN'T MEAN YOU HAVE TO DO IT

Many of us find ourselves headed down a certain career path because that's where our skills seem naturally to lead us. But just because we might have an aptitude for a particular kind of work doesn't mean it will necessarily be a good fit for us in the long haul. Think of all the bitter ex-child actors you've read about over the years.

I've worked with numerous professional athletes who decided to stop competing in professional sports and pursue other careers that were of greater interest to them or better matched their values at that time in their lives. Walking away from a pro sports career isn't easy. More often than not, such decisions are made without the support of coaches, team owners, agents, or family members who have become accustomed to the benefits of association with the professional athlete. Nevertheless, pros retire, and not always because of declining performance. Often it is simply because their goals have changed.

For a better career fit, don't just look to your skills but also to your interests and values. I don't mean to imply that it is absolutely necessary to select a career that delivers on all three counts—but if you could do that, why not?

If you've already made a good career for yourself that doesn't fulfill your interests and values, all is not lost. One idea would be to take a hard look at your work and ask yourself whether certain aspects of it are more in line with your interests and values than others. Then, over time, you can gradually shift your job responsibilities in that direction. Another possibility is to simply invest more of yourself in activities outside of work, such as sports, hobbies, or volunteer projects, that are a better match for your interests and values.

2. When I ask others to define the areas in which I am most
    skilled, they usually name the following:

    a) _____

    b) _____

    c) _____

3. The skills that I would most enjoy developing would be in
    the areas of:

    a) _____

    b) _____

    c) _____

CHAPTER 3

KNOW WHAT IT TAKES

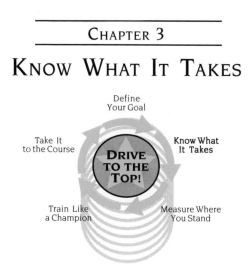

BEFORE READING THIS CHAPTER, PLEASE READ THE STATEMENTS BELOW. Using a one-to-five scale (five being very descriptive, and one being not very descriptive) rate each item as it applies to you.

_____ 1. I have a very clear understanding of the factors that most drive results in my business—the "necessary essentials."

_____ 2. I spend the majority of my time and energy on the "necessary essentials."

_____ 3. I delegate the necessary non-essentials (tasks that are necessary, but not critical) to others.

_____ 4. I do not get bogged down by low-priority activities and tasks that limit the time that I spend on high-priority items.

_____ 5. I surround myself with resources and tools that contribute greatly to my business results.

_____ 6. I have direct experience in my field of play that provides me with knowledge of what it takes to succeed.

Add up the scores of your six responses. A score of 24 or higher indicates that you "Know What It Takes" to drive results in your field of play. This chapter will try to give you some additional skills to further refine that knowledge. If you scored lower than 24, then as you read on, make note of the actions you can take to better understand exactly what's required to succeed in your business.

Deciding what you want to achieve is only a first step, of course, and in some ways it's the easiest. Figuring out how you're going to get there can be a much bigger challenge.

What top athletes want is to perform at a world-class level, especially when it counts most, in competition. While that's a worthy goal for anyone to work toward, it's also very vague. So athletes go a step further and break their performance down into its essential elements, creating what amounts to a series of sub-goals. Then they work systematically on each of those, especially the ones they know they're weakest at.

Professional golfers, for example, understand that to perform at a world-class level they have to shoot low scores—and to do this they must hit fairways, hit greens in regulation, get up-and-down, and make putts.[1] More precisely, they know that in order to compete on the PGA Tour these days they must maintain a scoring average of 71 or below, hit about 62 percent of the fairways, and 64 percent of the greens in regulation, and average approximately 1.79 putts per green that they hit in regulation. Those are benchmarks taken from data collected on the PGA Tour in 2007.

The world of business has its own ideas of what's essential in terms of performance. If you're in sales or manufacturing, for example, you may have a set of quotas to make. If you're running a company or a division of one, the goal might be a certain level of market share or profitability. Often the goals aren't as easily quantified as that, and sometimes they aren't very well communicated, but that doesn't mean you aren't being judged on whether or not you achieve them. Even if you don't know what it takes for you to be considered a top performer in your job, you can bet that your boss (or your boss's boss) has some definite thoughts on the subject.

So whether you're an athlete, a businessperson, or in any other endeavor, the key to achieving your goal is the same: (1) know what you want, (2) know what you have to do to achieve it, (3) know all the pieces that go into that, and (4) work like crazy on the areas where you don't measure up.

FOCUS ON THE ESSENTIALS

As I will probably say again and again throughout this book, world-class athletes and coaches spend the majority of their time doing things that are essential to driving performance. They recognize the importance of eliminating weaknesses in critical areas that are essential to their success. And they learn to be ruthless in not wasting their precious time on the things that aren't.

When somebody like Phil Mickelson goes to a golf tournament, he has to gas up his private jet for the trip, arrange for a hotel room, book transportation from the airport to the hotel, and so forth. He'll also have to figure out how he's going to invest all the money he's probably going to take home when that tournament is over.

I just named four activities that are completely necessary for a professional athlete like Phil Mickelson to do. But how many of them do you think he actually does himself? If he's smart about it, he probably won't do any of them.

While it may be necessary that someone does those things, it's not essential that *he* does them. Professional athletes, and businesspeople who become champions in their own fields, spend the bulk of their time working on the things that are most essential.

They delegate or find other ways to get things done that are necessary but less essential. Ask yourself, how well do you do that? And what can you do to do it better?

Suppose I asked you, "What's the single most essential thing Phil Mickelson should be doing with his time?" What would your answer be?

Probably that he should be hitting a ball with a stick at a target. If he's spending time hitting a ball with a stick at a target, either in practice or in tournament play, then he's doing the one thing that is most essential for him to stay at the top of his game.

> CHAMPIONS SPEND THE BULK OF THEIR TIME WORKING ON THE THINGS THAT ARE MOST ESSENTIAL.

What's the equivalent of hitting a ball with a stick at a target in your industry? If you're in sales, for example, maybe it's getting in front of prospects, speaking to customers, spending face-to-face time with people who are either going to become your customers or who will refer you to other people who will be. Now ask yourself what percent of your day do you spend doing that?

I work closely with a number of financial firms that employ wholesalers to distribute their products to the public via financial advisors in various channels: wire houses, independent firms, and banks. The goal of the wholesaler is simple: Sell! Sell mutual funds, variable annuities, life insurance, pension plans, etc.—and sell a lot of them! Within any given firm, the product being sold by the wholesalers is the same, yet some wholesalers sell a lot of it and others do not. Why? Because the top-producing wholesalers focus on what's essential. They spend their time "hitting a ball with a stick at a target."

In other words, the top salespeople spend their time doing the activities most likely to drive sales, namely: (1) meeting with financial advisors who have sold their product in the past, (2) identifying and meeting with new advisors who have the interest and ability to distribute their product, (3) effectively communicating the value proposition of their product, and (4) teaching financial advisors how to effectively sell their products to the end-user client.

It's not that there aren't a million other things that the wholesaler could be spending his or her time on. Just ask the poor performer who is spending too much time organizing expense receipts, talking on the phone with friends, getting lost in traffic on the way to a new branch, or meeting with advisors who have little or no opportunity to sell the products the wholesaler has to offer.

Before we get into the specific steps, I'd like to share some anecdotes from the worlds of golf and business that underscore the difference between how world-class performers approach these challenges and how the average person might.

When Greg Norman was the No. 1 player in the world, I had an opportunity to talk to him about his practice habits. Even though he'd already achieved more than most golfers ever dream of, Norman was still arriving at the golf course 20 minutes before sunrise, seven days a week. That gave him exactly 20 minutes for stretching exercises, which he did in the parking lot, using the bumper of his car, with his headlights on. After that he'd literally practice from sunrise to sunset. And as if that wasn't enough for the day, he'd go to the gym to work out.

I asked him, "When you get to the range, what do you work on?"

He didn't hesitate in answering, "I spend the bulk of my time working on the things that cost me the most strokes in competition," what I often refer to as an individual's weakest, most essential gaps.

Photo by Jacqueline Duvoisin, *Sports Illustrated*

"I spend the bulk of my time working on the things that cost me
the most strokes in competition." —*Greg Norman*

Now, contrast that to another player, whose name I won't use for obvious reasons. He'd been out of college for three or four years and was training in hopes of getting on the PGA Tour. He called me one day because he wasn't achieving the results he wanted and he couldn't figure out why. I asked him to send me some data on his performance so I could benchmark him in various skill areas against players already on the PGA Tour. (I'll explain this benchmarking process and how you can use it in Chapter 4.) Once I'd reviewed his data, it was clear that while his driving was strong enough to qualify him for the Tour, his putting, chipping, and pitching was costing him way too many strokes.

During one of our follow-up conversations, I asked him how much he practiced, and he said, "A good three to four days a week, two to three hours a day."

It was immediately clear that there was a fundamental difference between this struggling PGA Tour hopeful and Greg Norman. He was practicing 12 hours a week at most, and thinking that was more than adequate, while Norman was putting in nearly 60 hours…five times as much.

But an even more telling difference emerged from the next question I asked him. "Of those two to three hours you practice, how much time do you spend working on your short game?"

"About 30 minutes," he told me.

"And what are you doing for the rest of the time?" I asked.

"Usually," he said, "I'm hitting my driver."

In other words, here was a player who wasn't practicing much, and when he did practice he was just doing more of what he was already good at, not working on the part of his game that desperately needed help.

A lot of us are like that. It's human nature. We like to do the things we're good at more than the things that give us trouble. And yet, we stand to benefit the most by working on that latter group. The trick is to teach ourselves to look beyond the short-term, immediate gratification that we experience when we are working on our strengths. When we work on something that we are good at, we see positive results during practice. In golf, for instance, if you are a good putter and you head to the green to practice putting, you will likely make a lot of putts. As you do, you reinforce an already well-developed skill, enjoy the experience, and build confidence (if only in your putting).

Meanwhile, the parts of your game that are costing you the most strokes on the golf course continue to be neglected. Why? It is because if you were to work on them instead of putting, your experience might be quite different. Chances are, you'd be hitting more bad shots than good ones, at least initially, coping with the negative emotions that accompany the bad shots, and exposing your weakness to anyone who might walk by. Working on our weaknesses isn't always comfortable or easy, but it is essential.

In the world of business I see the same tendency. Salespeople who are already excellent at presenting the features and benefits of a product continue developing their pitch. But while they are doing that, they may be neglecting the inefficiencies in their time and territory-management skills that limit the number of prospects they see each day. As a result, their well-honed pitch doesn't reach nearly the audience that it might, and their sales fall far short of their true potential.

This need to focus is important when we are training to do our jobs better. It's also equally important to allow us to wisely choose not to do some things because they won't get us any closer to our ultimate goal.

Here, for example, is Bill Gates, arguably the Tiger Woods of the software world, explaining in a *Newsweek* interview a few years ago, how things worked at Microsoft: "We never waste a lot of time

Photo by China FotoPress, *Getty Images*

"We never waste a lot of time talking about what we're doing well....
Every meeting is about 'Sure, we won in seven of the categories,
but what about that eighth category?'"—*Bill Gates*

talking about what we're doing well. . . . Every meeting is about 'Sure, we won in seven of the categories, but what about that eighth category?'"

One of the most accomplished salespeople I've ever worked with, John Marshall of AIG SunAmerica, expressed a similar commitment to focus when I asked him about the secrets of his success. John told me, "It is important to make sure I am doing revenue-producing activities during revenue-producing hours. So, during the hours of eight a.m. to seven p.m., I am constantly asking myself, 'Is what I'm doing *right now* driving revenue?'"

If I know John, the answer is almost invariably yes. And the reason for that is his intense focus.

LINK YOUR EFFORTS TO THE RESULTS YOU WANT

Top performers learn to focus their efforts on well-defined, intended results: to win the Masters, to get promoted, to double their income, to retire by a certain age, and so forth. They go to great pains to make sure that their daily efforts are directly linked to their intended results. They don't want to waste time on things that may, on the surface, have some appeal (such as being quick or easy to accomplish), but in the long run don't move them any closer to their desired goal. They learn to say "no," both to themselves and to others.

I am often asked during golf workshops, "What percent of golf is mental?" I respond by saying, "Not as much as many sports psychologists would like you to believe." I have a saying that I share with many of the tour pros with whom I work: "If you aren't good, you'll soon be mental!" Meaning, in golf, the presence of skill supersedes mental toughness. Positive thinking only goes so far— and, in performance arenas, it doesn't go very far at all if you are not skilled. The level of confidence that we bring with us into any performance endeavor is directly related to the level of skill that we have achieved. The more skill we have, the more confidence we'll have, and thus, the less "mental" we will be.

I recall a PGA Advanced Teaching workshop that I was co-teaching, along with Butch Harmon, ranked No. 1 among *Golf Digest*'s Best Teachers in America. Butch said to me during a break, "It's nice to finally meet a psychologist who gets it. Too many of you mental guys imply that if a player can visualize it, they can do it. And that just isn't the case. It takes a lot of work and practice." In his coaching of the best players in the game (Tiger Woods, Phil Mickelson, Greg Norman, Natalie Gulbis, Adam Scott), Butch knows that he must focus on the essential drivers of performance in golf. And as much as sports psychologists would like those to be "mental" in

> IF YOU AREN'T GOOD, YOU'LL SOON BE MENTAL.

nature, they are not. They are the essential skills of golf—ball striking, putting, total driving, and short-game skills—all of which are developed through one critical process—practice!

As the great business guru Peter Drucker once put it, "There is nothing so useless as doing efficiently that which should not be done at all."

In business terms, it may help to think of this as your return on investment. The investment in this case is your time, a resource that's both finite and precious. If you're a manager or business owner, you'll need to think not only about your own time but the working time of everyone who reports to you or works for you.

So before you take on any new activity, always ask yourself the following questions:

- *Will doing this have a direct impact on the result I want?*
- *Why am I considering doing this at this time? (If it isn't because of a positive effect it will have on my intended result, why am I even considering it?)*
- *Are there other things that I should be considering doing that are more essential to achieving my intended result?*

It pays to review your current routines periodically, as well. Are you spending time, money, or energy on things that will not have a significant impact on your ability to achieve the result you want? If so, then get rid of them.

Performance is a bottom-line business. Becoming a champion is all about the eventual results.

S.P.E.R.T.S: THE SIX FACTORS THAT DRIVE RESULTS

Focusing your attention on the results you want is one key to becoming a top performer. However, focusing on results does not alone ensure that you will achieve success. You must also define and manage the factors that drive such results. These critical drivers can be remembered by the acronym, S.P.E.R.T.S.— Skills, Processes, Experience, Resources, Tools, and Strategies. (Yes, I know that acronym is a little corny, but believe me, you're more likely to remember it than if it was W.G.H.Q.X. or something.)

Skills

In golf, tour players must develop ball control skills in their long-game and in their short-game. They must be able to drive the ball in the fairway, hit greens with their approach shots, and make putts. These skills are critical. Without them, a player simply cannot compete.

When Tiger Woods first came on the PGA Tour scene, veteran players questioned whether he would live up to the hype that had preceded him. Would Tiger's dominance in the amateur ranks continue once he was playing with the big boys? It wasn't long before Woods raised the bar and the eyebrows of his PGA Tour competitors. One of them put it this way to me, "I've played with a lot of guys out here. You play with John Daly and you say to yourself, 'Boy, does he ever hit it far!' You play with Fred Funk and he never misses a fairway. Brad Faxon makes every putt he looks at. Everyone has their strength, but they also have some visible weaknesses. What's so amazing about Tiger is that he has no weakness. He is the best ball striker that I've ever seen, he is the best putter, he has the best short-game, and has a better mind than any guy out here. He has the entire package!"

In any performance endeavor, you must strive to master a core set of skills. Master all of them, and you're likely to dominate. To become a top performer in whatever you do, you must first be able to define the skills that are critical to success in your field of play.

In sales, for example, your critical skills might include gaining access to new customers or communicating a value proposition. If you're a banker, it may be directly assisting customers or supervising tellers. If you're a physician, diagnosing illness and prescribing treatment would be at the top of the list.

Take a moment here and list the three skills you consider most essential in your line of work or any other area of your life where you want to become a top performer. Don't concern yourself whether these are skills you've developed to a high level or ones you still need to work on. We'll get to that later in the book.

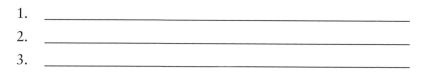

1. _____

2. _____

3. _____

Processes

Processes are the methods or systems you use to get things accomplished. In golf, pros have processes that they use to develop their skills, to warm up for a round, to prepare for a shot, to read a putt, and at the end of the day, to evaluate their performance. Top performers make sure that these processes are intentional, efficient, and repeatable.

In business, we have processes, too, such as scheduling our week, servicing accounts, paying bills, running meetings, creating budgets, filling out expense reports, and so forth. The champions in business identify, streamline, and perfect the processes that are essential to their performance.

As a consultant, I've had the opportunity to shadow hundreds of business professionals as they went about their jobs day-to-day. A common denominator among the best of them has been their attention to process. They turn the simple day-to-day activities into automated routines. As a result, their work lives become more efficient and more productive, and their successes more predictable.

Several years ago, I spent some days on the job and on the road with Bill Stubblefield. Bill is a mutual-fund wholesaler who has achieved the status of No. 1 producing salesperson at three different firms during the course of his 20-plus year career. By the end of the second day of our travels it became clear to me why Bill was so successful. He had turned every step of the sales process into a repeatable, masterful routine. That included how he gathered information from a client, delivered presentations, communicated with his assistant, and followed up with his customers.

Bill even had a process for how he packed his suitcase. He said to me, "You can judge the quality of a wholesaler by the size of his suitcase." By that he meant, the bigger the suitcase, the more suits, the more days on the road, the more clients seen, and—as an end result—the more sales.

I'll get more into how top performers turn best practices into routines in Chapter 6, *Take It to the Course.*

So, what are the critical processes that drive performance in your field of play? What processes are most essential? See if you can list three.

1. _____

2. _____

3. _____

Experience

In the world of golf it's well-known that there's no replacement for experience. Be paired with Tiger Woods coming down the stretch on a Sunday, and you will quickly learn the value of experience. Woods has been there so many times that he has a distinct advantage over all challengers. As a matter of fact, Woods won 13 of 13 (yes, 100 percent) of the major championships that he led after 54 holes. Yes, experience matters!

In many demanding arenas of life, experience is critical. My father retired from the Coast Guard as an officer after serving over 20 years. At certain points in his career, he found himself reporting to commanding officers who had much more book knowledge than he did but who hadn't spent anywhere near as much time at sea.

My father once told me about a particular time during an intense storm, a helmsman fell overboard into the rough waters. At the time, my father was the Officer on Deck (in charge on the bridge) and when he heard, "Man overboard—port side" come over the speaker system, he reacted immediately with "Left full rudder!" in order to turn the screws of the propeller away from the sailor in the water.

It was during times like these that my father confirmed the value of experience and the ability to react instinctively to an emergency. He also noted that, on such occasions, the commanding officer, who often had more academic credentials but much less sea time, would readily request information from and delegate tasks to those who had "been there before." Even military personnel, who abide strictly by the chain of command, recognize the value of experience and utilize it.

Obviously, experience isn't something we can gain overnight. Experience takes time. But top performers know that they can accelerate the process. Remember my conversation with Greg Norman earlier in this chapter? Why do you think he hit golf balls from sunrise to dark, seven days of the week? It was because that process gave him more experience. He probably hit more golf balls in a year than many players hit in a decade. He was packing a decade's worth of ball-hitting experience into a single year.

As a general rule, the more we do of something, (unless we're doing it wrong) the better we get at it.

So it is with business. Ever wonder why so many fabled business leaders have prided themselves on getting to the office by six a.m. or some other ungodly hour? Yes, a lot of them have been driven workaholics and not necessarily happy or well-rounded people. If you asked them, they would probably tell you they worked long hours simply because they got more done that way. But there was another benefit, one that even they might not have been aware of; the more they worked the more experience they were gaining from every work day. A man or woman, who puts in 10 hours a day instead of eight, will have racked up close to 500 extra hours of experience by the end of a typical year. And if they keep at it each year, they will pull farther and farther ahead of their less-ambitious peers. At the end of 10 years, they will have about 12.5 years of experience rather than just 10.

Not only that, but the more often we do certain tasks, the more efficient we become at doing them. Consider how long it took you to tie a shoe the first time you did it and how long it takes now. Or how long it takes you or me to change a car tire versus how fast an Indy 500 pit crew can do it? As we do more of something, we learn to do it faster, with less hesitation, and with less wasted motion. And that, in turn, allows us to accomplish even more in any given period of time.

I'm not saying that working longer hours is always a good thing. It can, as we all know, do enormous damage to a person's personal or family life. But it's a sacrifice that many top achievers choose to make and one more way to get an extra edge.

I believe there's an even better way, however. And that's to manage your time so that you spend more of it on tasks that will give you the skills and experience you need and less of it working on things that are less essential. That can be far more important than simply working longer hours.

In financial services firms, top-producing advisors are recognized by the amount of revenue they generate. Incentive trips, recognition clubs, bonuses, and other rewards are bestowed on million-dollar producers each year. Interestingly, very little attention is given to the question, "How much expense went into earning the million dollars?"

I've worked with advisors who generate $750,000 in revenue working 35 hours per week and employing one assistant. Yet those advisors often fly beneath the radar while the million-dollar producer who works 70 hour weeks and employs three assistants, gathers all the recognition. If these two advisors' businesses were publicly traded, which would you invest in? Which advisor do you think has figured out how to effectively allocate time?

Later in this book, we'll see how you can focus a greater portion of your effort on what's essential. Meanwhile, take a moment to list three types of experience that are most critical to your success. And next to each, make a note about what you can do to gain more experience in each of those areas.

1. _____

2. _____

3. _____

Resources

By "resources", I mean *human* resources. Elin Nordegren, Mark Steinberg, Steve Williams, Hank Haney, and Keith Klevens—do these names sound familiar? They are Tiger Woods' supporting cast—his wife, agent, caddie, coach, and trainer. Getting to the top of your field without the help of others is a difficult if not impossible task. Touring golf pros rely on many resources along their journey to the top—golf instructors, sports psychologists, fitness experts, attorneys, agents, club manufacturers, sponsors, and the list goes on.

I once asked the renowned CBS golf broadcaster and 1964 U.S. Open Champion Ken Venturi to comment on the resources that were most influential to his career as a professional golfer. He told me, "I was very fortunate. Having [Byron] Nelson teach me, and [Ben] Hogan take me under his wing—I mean to me it's like being taught by Michelangelo and Leonardo da Vinci."

As Johnny Miller, World Golf Hall of Fame inductee and later a successful broadcaster like Venturi, once remarked, "No one ever becomes a champion without help."

In business, too, we rely on our colleagues, bosses, subordinates, and outside experts when needed. Walt Disney, who built a business

Photo by Heinz Kluetmeier, *Sports Illustrated*

"No one ever becomes a champion without help." —*Johnny Miller*

empire out of a cartoon mouse, once observed, "It seems to me shallow and arrogant for any man in these times to claim he is completely self-made, that he owes all his success to his own unaided efforts. Many hands and hearts and minds generally contribute to anyone's notable achievements." Similarly, Ray Kroc, founder of McDonald's Corporation said "You're only as good as the people you hire." Champions at the top of any industry recognize the importance of all the people who have contributed to their accomplishments.

Part of the reason we rely on others is that none of us, no matter how good we are at what we do, is an expert at everything. The other important aspect is that by having other people that we can rely on to do what they do well, we are able to focus more of our time and attention on becoming the best at what we do.

To take a really absurd example, suppose that while nobody was paying attention, Tiger Woods snuck off and got himself a law degree. And while he was at it, he earned a degree in accounting. And at night he went to business school. Does anybody think that Tiger Woods should spend time writing up his own contracts, doing his own taxes, and serving as CEO of the PGA Tour? No, of course not, even if he happened to be pretty good at all three of those things. He's just too valuable doing what he's best at—dominating the game of golf.

What human resources would help you to succeed in your field of play? Which ones do you have in place already? Are there any gaps where you could still use help? Take a moment and list them here.

The human resources you already have to draw on:

1. _____

2. _____

3. _____

What other specific people could also be useful resources to you? (If you can't think of a particular person, what are the areas of expertise where you would like to find someone to help you?) You may want to consult the list you made in Chapter 1 of the people whose character traits you admire.

1. _____

2. _____

3. _____

Tools

Tools are the other resources you need to do your work effectively, the non-human ones. For the golfer, of course, these are clubs, shoes, balls, and all the rest of the pro shop paraphernalia. For the businessperson, it may be your laptop, your PDA, a critical piece of software, a company car, or whatever.

While it's a good idea not to get too hung up on tools (a $200 putter in the hands of a lousy golfer isn't going to magically start sinking 30-foot putts, and a $200 pen doesn't write up business any better than a $20 or even a $2 one), it's absolutely essential that you equip yourself with the tools you need. These tools should be of high quality, and you should adopt new and better ones as they come along.

And they do come along, often faster than we realize. Too many of us, myself included, are slow to identify and acquire the most up-to-date and effective tools of our trade. Typically, that's because we are comfortable with what we have, or just don't want to spend the money.

Recently I was playing golf with a friend of mine who owns and manages a club-fitting business. After playing the front nine, he pulled my driver out of my bag and said, "How long have you been playing this dinosaur, anyway?"

I quickly came to the defense of my club. "I love that club," I said. "I've had it about seven years."

My friend explained how much distance I was sacrificing on each tee shot by not taking advantage of more modern technology.

Once more I defended my position, saying, "Yeah, but I know where the ball goes with this one because I've been playing it for so long."

So my friend asked me simply to play the next nine holes with his driver and see what I thought.

Well, I hit every tee shot 20 to 30 yards farther and the ball traveled just as straight and just as consistently as it would have with my old club. (And no, I don't think it was a placebo effect, although as a psychologist that crossed my mind.)

Shame on me, I thought. I wasn't practicing what I preach about the need for up-to-date tools. Change can be a difficult thing, even for those of us who give speeches and write about it. By the way, I now own that club, bought it on the spot. And I will bet that I'll need to replace it with an even better one before another seven years has gone by.

In business, new tools are being developed and upgraded at warp speed these days. By the time we have finally made it through the user's manual of our laptop, cell phone, PDA, or client-management software (for those who ever actually consult the manual at all!) version 2.0 is being rolled out.

Does that mean we have to buy the new and supposedly improved version of every tool? I don't think so. A good rule is to determine whether the benefits will outweigh the time and expense involved in making the change. More often than not, it's been my experience that the upgrade was worth it, but certainly not always. Our tools, whether in sports or in business, are just that, tools. A tool is the means to an end (the results we want to achieve with the tool), not an end in itself.

The swift changes in technology offer a good example of the kind of blind spots all of us have in one area or another. How can we upgrade something if we aren't even aware that an upgrade exists? One thing I have come to realize over the years is that I often don't know what I don't know. So in the case of technology, each year I hire a technology consultant to come to my office and do an evaluation of my business. I spend several hours demonstrating what my office staff and I do on a daily basis, how we do it, and the tools we use. Then I ask one question, "If you were us, what tools would you be using that we are not?"

Inevitably, the consultant looks at me as if I am living in the dark ages. Then he or she asks, "Why aren't you using blank?"

"I didn't know about blank." I don't know what I don't know.

Champions recognize that they have blind spots. They take the extra steps to turn their head, look over their shoulder, and investigate what they would not otherwise see. And they aren't shy about seeking expert help where necessary.

In which areas of your business do you think you might have blind spots? (For example, it might be technology, diagnostics, prospecting strategies, client service systems, training, employee benefits, or any of a thousand other things.) Also ask yourself who (or what kind of firm) might be able to help you correct your blind spots. We'll call that your blind-spot optometrist. List them here:

My Possible Blind Spots

_____

_____

My Blind Spot Optometrist

_____

_____

Now, let's get back to the subject of tools. What tools do the top performers in your field of play use? If you don't know, observe or ask them. This is one secret of success almost everybody is more than happy to share.

Which tools do you need that you don't have, or that you may need to upgrade? List them here:

1. _____

2. _____

3. _____

Strategies

Golfing legend Jack Nicklaus dominated the major championships. He won a record 18 major titles, a number that many in golf wonder if even Tiger Woods will ever reach. (Woods was at 13 at the end of the 2007 season.) A key reason for Nicklaus' dominance at the Majors was his commitment to designing and executing a strategy that would give him the best possible chance of winning every time.

At Augusta National, home of the Masters Tournament, where Nicklaus won a record six green jackets, he demonstrated this commitment. He was known for playing many more practice rounds there than his competitors during the weeks prior to the tournament. And with each visit, Nicklaus would hone his strategy of how he was going to play the course. He would predetermine where to take risks and where to play it safe, what club to hit off each tee, how putts would break, how much a ball would release on greens, etc. Nicklaus understood that winning Majors was not only dependent on his considerable talent but on his ability to apply that talent within a predetermined, intentional game plan.

Is it any surprise that Tiger Woods would follow Nicklaus' lead? Woods started the 2007 PGA Tour season by saying, "My whole goal is to get ready for Augusta and prepare and make sure my game is peaking towards that."

Similarly, pro football and basketball teams have very well-defined strategies they use in playing offense and defense. They may have different strategies for certain opponents and alternate strategies to switch to when their customary strategy isn't working. Coaches may go into a game with a particular strategy, but if they are smart, there's enough flexibility in it to allow for changes during the course of the game. And if they aren't smart, they probably aren't going to last long at that level of coaching.

Businesses do their own form of strategic planning, of course, trying to forecast the likely demand for their products, the cost of labor, and many other variables. And smart individuals have their own strategic plans, whether that involves doing their current job more effectively, moving up in their organization, or moving on to another one.

Consider a salesperson, for example. His or her strategies might look like this:

- Schedule appointments with 5 new prospects each day
- Prioritize my time by level of prospect—spend 75 percent of my day with high-potential clients
- Focus my attention on obtaining repeat business from existing clients
- Increase my close ratio on opportunities by improving my execution of my sales process.

Or consider the owner of a new business. These might be appropriate strategies for him or her:

- Implement an automated client-management system to maintain and log customer contact

WHEN TO CHANGE STRATEGY, AND WHEN NOT TO

If you're dominating your game, there's little reason to change what you're doing; a tweak here and there, maybe, but certainly not a wholesale change. Except, that is, when the environment around you is changing in a way that is likely to affect whether your strategy will continue to work in the future. In that case, change can be a matter of survival.

Bear in mind that changing your strategy isn't always easy. In fact, the more successful you've been following a particular strategy; the more difficult it may be to change. But the fact that it's difficult doesn't make it any less essential.

In the ever-changing technology sector, Bill Gates recognized that change was difficult but essential even for a wildly successful organization like his. In a 1995 memo to his executive staff, he wrote, "This coming 'services wave' will be very disruptive. We have competitors who will seize on these approaches and challenge us; still, the opportunity for us to lead is very clear. We must recognize this change as an opportunity for us to take our offerings to the next level, compete in a manner commensurate with our industry responsibilities, and utilize our assets and our broad reach to reshape our business for the benefit of our products, our customers, our partners, and ourselves."

Jack Nicklaus may have put it even more succinctly when asked about U.S. players who didn't attempt to qualify for the British Open because they were uncomfortable with the courses. "That's the biggest bunch of rubbish I've ever heard," golf columnist Bill Nichols quoted him as saying. "The whole idea of golf is that you have to adapt your game to the course you are playing."

- Reduce overhead by outsourcing purchasing to a Web-based e-procurement provider
- Develop and provide value-added resources to be used by the sales team in furthering relationships with our top distributors

So, what strategies have you set for yourself? Which ones are working well at the moment and which aren't? And if you haven't given the matter much thought before, do so now. Then list the strategies you should be pursuing here:

1. _____

2. _____

3. _____

4. _____

[1] For non-golfers, these and other golf terms are defined in the Glossary (page 171).

CHAPTER 4

MEASURE WHERE YOU STAND

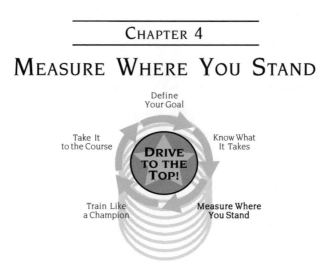

IN THE PRECEDING CHAPTERS WE TALKED ABOUT (1) defining your goals and (2) knowing what it takes to achieve those goals. Those two steps are relatively straightforward, and you may already have given them a lot of thought before you ever picked up this book.

The next step is one that is second nature to most top athletes but sometimes comes as a surprise to men and women in business, no matter how goal-oriented they may be: measuring where you stand.

In business, individuals often prematurely leap into planning before collecting the data necessary to make good decisions. Once they *know what it takes*, businesspeople frequently set strategic plans that focus on those factors, without first measuring their relative strengths and weaknesses.

Before proceeding, please read the statements below and consider how descriptive each one is of you. Using a one-to-five scale (five being very descriptive, and one being not very descriptive) rate each item as it applies to you.

_____ 1. I go beyond measuring just my outcomes and also measure the factors that contribute to my outcomes.

_____ 2. I know others who I can turn to for feedback on how I measure up against those considered to be the best in my business.

_____ 3. I have access to the measures of other successful individuals who provide an appropriate benchmark to which I can compare myself.

_____ 4. I use measurement to prioritize the factors that most contribute to my performance outcomes.

_____ 5. When I examine others who are performing at levels higher than me, I can pinpoint specifically what they are doing differently to achieve such results.

_____ 6. I can identify the top two or three things that I must improve to give me the greatest opportunity for improvement.

Take note of the items above that you ranked with a three or less. As you read on, consider what specific changes you can make in your behavior to improve your ability to measure where you stand.

Professional athletes and those determined to reach that level are constantly measuring themselves against the leaders in their field on a whole range of skills particular to their sport. Their goal is to find the gaps between what they can currently do in terms of a particular skill and what those top performers can do. You'll hear this referred to as "conducting a gap analysis." Then, through training, they can work on their weaker skills and attempt to bridge the gaps.

In my work with many tour players who aspire to be the next Tiger Woods or Annika Sorenstam, I've found that their No. 1 need is to measure where they stand relative to players who are already where they want to be. In most cases, tour pros who are in the middle of the pack know all too well that their scoring average is not yet up to par with their idols at the top of the money lists. However, what they do not know is precisely why. In particular, they don't know where they stand on each of the five factors that drive results, the S.P.E.R.T.S. (skills, processes, experience, resources, tools, and strategies) we discussed in the previous chapter.

Until these players know exactly where they stand, they are unable to establish an efficient, on-target training plan that will help them close the gap between their present situation and their ultimate goal.

DO MORE THAN KEEP SCORE

To measure where you stand in any competitive arena, you have to do more than just keep score. Think of your "score" as your measurable end-results within the arena where you currently compete. It might be the number of wins, market share, sales ranking, or any other broad measure that you and others track to determine who is "winning." While your score tells you something about your ultimate performance, it doesn't tell you much about how you got there, or about how you can do better in the future.

Have you ever worked for a manager who continually pushed you to achieve the next level but never offered any useful guidance on how to get there? He or she was paying attention to measures, but only to outcome measures, such as your year-to-date sales, monthly sales, or even weekly sales. If you happened to fall behind, the message you'd get is, "Pick it up. You're not hitting your goal."

Well, thanks for nothing. Telling someone they're not hitting a goal adds nothing to their knowledge. They can figure that out by themselves by, in this example, simply looking at the sales numbers.

What champions want to know isn't just the outcome, which they know anyhow, but how they're doing on the factors that drive their outcomes.

Imagine a tour player meeting with me and asking, "I'm in the middle of the pack on the PGA Tour, but one day I'd like to be competitive with Tiger Woods. What should I do?"

How much value would I bring to the relationship if my response was something like, "Well, I studied the data and Tiger won seven million dollars more than you last year and his 18-hole scoring average is 68.1, whereas yours was 70.1. What I want you to do is make seven million more and cut another two shots off your scoring average."

I think the player would look at me and think, "No kiddin', (or earthier words to that effect) Sherlock!"

What that player really needed and wanted to know is *why* he was giving up two shots. Without being able to measure that, I wouldn't be able to create a targeted, effective plan for improvement. What's more, with an answer like that, I would lose the player's respect and trust, the cornerstones of any coach/player relationship.

Jack Nicklaus once told his longtime coach, Jack Grout, "Each time we played, you made me learn something of why I was doing something and the mistakes I made. I think that is the greatest thing you ever did for me, because it allowed me to graduate from being dependent on you to being dependent on myself."

What a legend like Nicklaus valued most from his coach and mentor was knowing the *why*. If you are in management, do you provide your staffers with more than the score? If you are striving to be the Jack Nicklaus of your industry, do you have access to measures that will provide you and your team with the *whys* that tell why your scores are what they are?

To build strategic plans of any significant worth, champions go far beyond setting outcome goals. That's where some other measures come in. To really know where you stand, you must also:

1. Track your pertinent performance stats.
2. Establish best-in-the-business benchmarks.
3. Prioritize your most critical driver needs.

Here's what each of those steps involves and how you can make use of them in your own career.

1. Track your pertinent performance stats.

Your performance stats differ from your score in that they measure you on a number of dimensions and at a number of points. In golf, for example, your performance stats would include percentage of fairways hit, percentage of greens hit in regulation, percentage of up and downs, and number of putts hit per green in regulation. In sales, these performance stats might be dollars of sales per day, dollars of sales per customer, number of prospects seen per day, and percent of prospects who bought something. They aren't total sales year-to-date, which is merely your final score. By keeping accurate, relevant, and up-to-date performance stats, you can more effectively track your performance over time as well as compare your performance with that of colleagues or competitors who are performing at a higher level.

Champions want to be the best—and they become the best by dominating the most essential performance statistics that drive their competitive outcomes. As we discussed in Chapter 3, *Know What It Takes*, there are a number of easily defined factors (S.P.E.R.T.S.) that drive results. Within each of these S.P.E.R.T.S., top performers strive to measure where they stand against those who are outperforming them.

In golf, for example, PGA and LPGA pros benchmark themselves against the best of the best on a wide range of factors that are likely to make a difference in their results. These benchmarks range from hours of practice time to number of three-putts per round to clubhead speed, to average distance of a putt following their approach shots.

In business you should benchmark yourself against those you aspire to equal, and ideally, surpass. Let's take a closer look at how champions like Tiger Woods use benchmarking to elevate their game. Then we'll look at how you can apply the same principles in your work.

When he was only 13, Tiger Woods became a scratch golfer. (For those of you who don't play golf, that means, in its least technical sense, that he shot par or better, usually 72 or lower for a round of 18 holes.) By 15 he became the youngest player to win the U.S. Junior Amateur Championship, and at 18 he was the youngest man to ever win the U.S. Amateur Championship. Before he turned 21, Woods had won a total of three U.S. Amateur Championships, and had become Rookie of the Year on the PGA Tour.

Wouldn't you like to know how someone who achieved such great results did it? The answer is that rather than focusing on the results, Woods dominated the essential drivers of results in the sport of golf. He did that as a junior, and he continued to do it as a professional on the PGA tour. The next year, still just 21 years old, Woods was the leading money winner on the PGA tour.

In other words, Woods dominated at age 15, age 18, age 21—and he will likely continue his dominance as long as he continues to measure and focus on the essential drivers of his results.

Top athletes like Woods measure where they stand against their competition and strive to achieve No. 1 status—not only in dollars won and number of championships, but more significantly on the measures that drive these outcomes. Following are a few relative performance stats for Tiger Woods that demonstrate this point.

Tiger Woods' Relative PGA Tour Ranking
1997 to 2000

Outcome Stats	1997	1998	1999	2000
Annual Earnings	1st	4th	1st	1st
Scoring Average	2nd	2nd	1st	1st
Performance Stats				
Greens in Regulation	4th	30th	1st	1st
Total Driving	9th	14th	1st	1st
Putts per Green in Regulation	60th	147th	24th	2nd
Scrambling Percentage	68th	12th	10th	3rd

In 1997, Woods finished the season in the No. 1 position on the PGA Tour's money list. The following year Woods and his coach, Butch Harmon, were criticized by some in the sports media for changing Tiger's golf swing. Why, the critics wanted to know, would anyone change something that was obviously working? Hadn't Butch Harmon ever heard the famous phrase, "If it ain't broke, don't fix it"?

The behind-the-scenes reality was that both Woods and Harmon knew exactly what they were doing. As you can see from that chart, although Woods was No. 1 on the Tour in earnings he did not dominate the major performance stats that drive dominance on the Tour. He ended the season No. 9 in the world in total driving and 60th and 68th in putting and scrambling respectively. And you can be certain that numbers like those are absolutely unacceptable to someone like Tiger Woods, who strives to be No. 1 in every category.

I remember watching a Golf Channel broadcast in which Woods, Harmon, and host Peter Kessler discussed Woods' determination to be the best. Harmon pointed to Woods, who was sitting beside

Photo by Fred Vuich, *Sports Illustrated*

"I want to be No. 1." —*Tiger Woods*

him, and said, "He led the Tour in greens in regulation and he hit, I think, 73 percent of his fairways. He says, 'I want to be top 20 in fairways.'"

Woods quickly interjected, "That's what he says. I want to be No. 1. I want to beat Fred Funk."

For those in the know, the comment was a sort of an inside joke. Funk is often teased by other players who say that he will always lead the driving accuracy stats because he doesn't hit the ball far enough to reach the rough. Joke or not, note that Woods didn't hesitate to say that he wanted to be No. 1. And that's not just in money won but in all the stats that contribute to that outcome.

So, as you can see from the data, if you only measure where you stand on outcomes, you will fail to discover the S.P.E.R.T.S. that are keeping you from reaching your upper potential. However, if, like Woods, you measure where you stand on the essential performance stats, you will discover that even if you are No. 1 in outcomes, there is apt to be plenty of room for additional gains. Yes, even someone like Tiger Woods can get better.

In fact, here's an interesting piece of data that relates to the measures in the chart on page 82. As you can see, in 1997 Tiger Woods was ranked No.1 in earnings. By the way, David Duval was ranked No. 2, and Woods surpassed Duval's earnings by just under $200,000 that year. Two years later, in 1999, Tiger Woods was again No. 1 in earnings, and, yes, David Duval was again No. 2. So the players in the top two positions on the Tour had not changed. However, their relative performance stats had. In 1999, as you'll see in the chart, Woods moved his rankings to No. 1 in greens in regulation, No. 1 in total driving, No. 10 in scrambling, and No. 24 in putting.

Now, if you're in business, what kind of impact do you think an improvement like that in your performance stats would have on revenue? Well, let's just say "significant." In 1999, Woods surpassed the Tour's next best player, Duval, by nearly three million dollars. Even more impressive, a year later, Woods almost "ran the table" by taking top honors in earnings, scoring average, greens in regulation, and driving statistics…and he finished second in putting and third in scrambling. Wow.

Phil Mickelson had moved into the No. 2 spot in earnings that year, and would you believe that Woods surpassed Mickelson's earnings by a whopping $4,441,864?

The message here is simple: Dominate the essential performance stats (the drivers) of your game, and you will dominate the outcomes. Setting outcome goals is only the first step in using measurement to take your performance to another level. You must then take the additional step of setting goals for those essential drivers that are making the greatest contribution to your outcomes.

What are the drivers that contribute most to your current outcome goals? If you are in sales, for example, it may be the number of proposals, closing percentage, or average size of a sale. If you're in sales management, it may be the rate of improvement of your sales team or the speed at which new hires can take it to the street. Or it may be your ability to provide your sales team with data that show where they stand relative to one another or to your competitors.

Let's look deeper now at how you can use these measures, regardless of the type of business you're in.

2. Establish best-in-the-business benchmarks.

Once you have established a system for tracking your pertinent performance stats, you then want to compare your stats with those of the best of your business. Conducting that kind of gap analysis will allow you to determine where you should spend your energy, time, and resources. When you more closely examine the areas that are essential to top performance in your arena, what are the most significant differences between you and those who are established champions?

When I first started consulting with touring pros on the PGA and LPGA Tours, there was not much data that was readily available. So I would ask the caddies of the players with whom I worked to track certain measures during the round—fairways hit, greens in regulation, number of putts per hole, distance of a putt after a short-game shot, etc.

Initially, even after collecting such data on a given player all I could do was compare that data to where the player was earlier in the season or against similar data I'd compiled on some of the other players with whom I worked. Over time I populated my database with information on more and more players and had a useful and valued benchmark. Today the PGA Tour recognizes the value of data (to the players, the coaches, the media, and the fans). On the PGA Tour, shots are measured by laser, and calculations are made instantaneously for dozens

> DOMINATE THE
> ESSENTIAL
> PERFORMANCE
> STATS (THE
> DRIVERS)
> OF YOUR GAME,
> AND YOU WILL
> DOMINATE
> THE OUTCOMES.

of critical measures—length of drive, distance from the hole, length of putts, and so forth. With this data it's possible to determine where a player is strong and where he is weak, relative to the PGA Tour field. There is no longer any need for guesswork. The Tour has institutionalized the value of measurement and benchmarks.

Amazingly, this is not the case in many business settings. Goals are often established using what I call "monkey math." This involves calculations so basic a reasonably intelligent monkey could do them. This kind of goal-setting leads to absurdities like, "Let's add 10 percent to last year's goal," when that 10 percent has no basis in reality beyond being a nice round number.

Just as bad is the, "Let's see what Wall Street wants and promise it," approach, all the while ignoring economic conditions, the competitive landscape, the cost of goods, and a host of other factors that actually drive a company's results.

If you have been the unfortunate victim of such practices, you know how frustrating it can be to have an outcome goal thrust upon you and not be given the resources and tools that will allow you to accomplish it.

On the other hand, many successful businesses, like the PGA Tour, establish benchmarks to gain insight into where individuals stand relative to their peers, their previous performance, their established goals, and their competition. Knowing what is achievable is very important to anyone who wants to reach his or her utmost potential. PGA Tour players benchmark themselves against the stats of Tiger Woods, LPGA players against Annika Sorenstam, and ATP tennis players against Roger Federer.

Imagine if you were coaching Tiger Woods or Phil Mickelson, currently the No. 1 and No. 2 players in the world, respectively, and you had no benchmarks to tell them where they stood relative to their peers and to one another. To provide champions of this caliber with advice based on hunches, guesswork, or intuition would be ludicrous when you have the ability to conduct a gap analysis using established benchmarks.

Take a look at this table showing the relative rankings of Woods and Mickelson in May 2007:

Tiger Woods vs. Phil Mickelson
May 2007 - Relative PGA Tour Ranking

Outcome Stats	Woods	Mickelson
Annual Earnings	1st	2nd
Scoring Average	1st	4th
Performance Stats		
Greens in Regulation	4th	45th
Total Driving	124th	60th
Putts per Green in Regulation	9th	1st
Scrambling Percentage	66th	51st

As you can see, Woods led Mickelson in earnings and scoring average, but he only led him in one of the four major performance stats that drive results on the PGA Tour. These stats demonstrate how critical "greens in regulation" is to success on the Tour. More important in terms of strategy, they also show how these two players would focus their training plans. You can bet that both of them were doing whatever it took to improve their total driving and scrambling rankings.

Interestingly, much of the talk in the golf media, as I write this, concerns Mickelson's recent decision to let go of his longtime swing coach Rick Smith and hire Butch Harmon, Tiger Woods' former coach. The coaching change creates some side plots that the golf media just love: Can Butch take Phil to the top of the game as he did with Greg Norman and Tiger Woods? Is Rick Smith really the reason Phil's ball striking wasn't better? Will Phil finally step up his game and challenge the dominance of Tiger? Was Tiger's decision to let Butch go and begin working with Hank Haney wise?

Moving forward, the answers to these questions will emerge in the data. The data certainly support Mickelson's decision to make a

Photo by Robert Beck, *Sports Illustrated*

"I feel that now is the time to go in a new direction with Butch Harmon on my long game. I went to Rick Smith as a friend and asked for his understanding of this decision and he's been very supportive of it." —*Phil Mickelson*

shift in strategy. What's that phrase—"Insanity is doing the same thing over and over and expecting different results!" If Mickelson and Harmon can implement a training plan that targets and improves Phil's "greens in regulation" and "driving" stats, it would very likely have a positive effect on the larger outcomes—annual earnings and scoring average.

Note that Mickelson's decision to make a change was data-based, not personal. He isn't one to jump from one coach to another hoping to find a quick fix as evidenced by his commitment to Rick Smith for an extended period of time. However, for whatever reason, it appears that they hit a wall. And champions would much rather spend time climbing walls than banging into them!

Both Woods and Mickelson have made some tough coaching changes that, at a personal level, are very difficult. In business we have to make decisions that are equally tough. And even though they may be personally difficult, they do not have to be "personal." By using best-in-the-business benchmarks, we are able to look at our performance and the contributions of others with far greater objectivity.

Establishing these benchmarks not only tells you what's possible but allows you to pinpoint your greatest, most essential gaps. Figuring out which of these gaps to work on first is the next step in our process.

3. Prioritize your most critical driver needs.

Once you have collected your performance stats and benchmarked them against the best in your business, you can then begin the task of prioritizing what you most urgently need to work on to take your performance to the next level.

The issue once again becomes: "What is essential?" As we've discussed, it is essential that all efforts link directly to your intended results. In order to measure the cause and effect linkages that contribute most to our success, we must be keeping score, tracking pertinent performance stats, benchmarking against the best in the business, and prioritizing our most critical driver needs.

In golf, there are many critical drivers of a player's ultimate score and finish in a tournament, from putting to chipping to hitting fairways. Once players have gathered their performance stats and compared them to the established Tour benchmarks, they can prioritize the critical drivers that are most separating them from the best in the business.

For example, if a mini-tour player has been unsuccessful at qualifying for the PGA Tour, simply knowing that he is not good enough doesn't help. He must know where the most essential gaps are between him and the PGA Tour standards for each of the critical drivers that most affect success on the Tour. Below is an example of a gap analysis between a mini-tour player's critical drivers and those of a player on the PGA Tour.

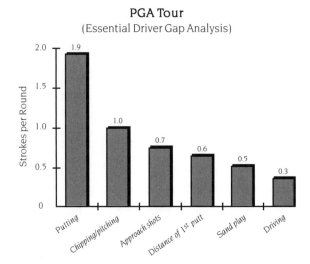

PGA Tour
(Essential Driver Gap Analysis)

Adapted from Tour Pro Stats software developed by David Tierney

The essentials driver gap analysis charted on page 91 quantifies the difference between a mini-tour player and a tour player on six critical skills in golf. In business circles, such an analysis is referred to as a histogram or a Pareto chart. Each bar is an indicator of the number of strokes per round that the mini-tour player gives up to a model PGA Tour player. We can then prioritize, based on "strokes per round," the critical drivers offering the greatest room for improvement. In this case, the player's biggest gaps are

> IT IS ESSENTIAL THAT ALL EFFORTS LINK DIRECTLY TO YOUR INTENDED RESULTS.

putting along with chipping and pitching. If you aren't a golfer and don't know what those terms mean, don't worry about it. They are simply skills that players use when they are trying to get the ball in the hole when it's on or near the putting green. The more important point here is to understand the notion of a gap analysis, which can be used for many things besides golf.

Measuring where this player stands lays the groundwork for making decisions about what the player should focus on as he strives to master the essential I'll discuss in the next chapter, *Train Like a Champion*. Not to get ahead of ourselves here, but since the illustration is handy, where do you think the mini-tour player should invest the greatest training effort?

If you answered "the skills with the biggest potential for payback," you're absolutely right. And he should put his least effort toward developing skills that correlate the least with his on-course outcomes or show the smallest gap between his performance and that of a touring pro. Yes, it might be nice to improve those, too, but the potential benefit is too small to worry about, at least until he's narrowed the big, high-payback gaps.

Note that in order to focus on your greatest, most essential skills, you must consider two things: (1) which skills really are most essential—that is, have the most significant correlation with the final results, and (2) which of these essential skills are measurably the weakest. For instance, in golf, the three most essential skills are hitting greens in regulation, putting, and total driving—in that order. It's nice to be skilled in the area of sand saves as well, but much less essential since players are in a bunker only one to two times per round.

You would think that the concept of minimizing the greatest, most essential gaps in your game would be easily understood and embraced. Surprisingly, many golfers and businesspeople not only don't follow that concept, but they do just the opposite!

People tend to work on what they are already good at. Golfers who drive the ball well, love bombing drivers on the range. Businesspeople who are great visionaries love to generate new ideas, new products, and new strategic directions. Why? It's because that's where they're most comfortable. Practicing what we're already good at gives us a sense of accomplishment, confidence, and self-assurance. Our strengths remind us that we are good at something and make us feel successful. However, in many professions a weakness in an essential driver will simply offset a strength in another, with the net result being average performance. And champions aren't looking for average performance. They want to dominate!

In 2002, soon after Tiger Woods left his coach Butch Harmon, many people criticized Woods for abandoning a teacher who contributed so much to his success. Shortly after their split, I happened to ask Jack Nicklaus what he thought about it. Nicklaus stuck with one teacher for much of his career, so I expected that he'd be critical of Tiger's decision. Yet, he told me that sometimes a player has to do what he has to do in order to keep improving. He

It's All in the Interpretation

Recently I was meeting with a PGA Tour player during the off-season to review his performance stats. Before I offered my analysis, I asked him, "What aspect of your game is the weakest and thus costing you the most strokes in competition?"

He immediately said, "My putting. I just don't make enough birdie putts." He pointed out that his stats for "Birdie Average" (measured by average number of birdies per round) were weak.

However, poor putting is not always the cause of a lack of birdies! After examining his putting in more depth, I pointed out to him that his percentage of putts holed-out from various distances on the green was actually quite good.

So, why wasn't he making more birdies? Well, his stat for "Average Distance of Birdie Putts" was weak, suggesting that, although he was an excellent putter, he rarely hit the ball close enough to the hole to have a legitimate chance of making it.

To the right is the player's gap analysis, which displays the strokes per round that he scores above/worse than (+) or below/better than (-) a model PGA Tour player for each essential driver.

As you can see, his putting was better than the model player; however, his "Distance of 1st Putt" was worse (costing him more than 0.5 shots per round). Interestingly, his "Approach Shots" (measured by the number of greens he hit in regulation) were excellent. How could it be that he was good enough to hit plenty of greens, yet he didn't hit his share of shots close to the hole?

As we discussed these results, I asked, "How often do you fire at a pin with your short irons and wedges?" He responded, "Not too often—don't have to. Why make a stupid bogey by missing the pin

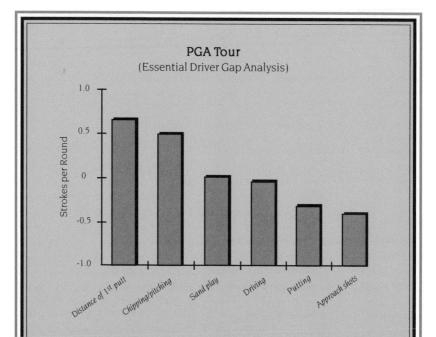

on the short side? I'd rather roll in a 20-footer for birdie and, at worse, make par."

In this case, the player's conservative strategy was supported by his statistics as well. If you examine his gap analysis a bit closer, you will see that his Chipping/Pitching was relatively weak. In an effort to avoid the negative consequences of this weakness (i.e. "stupid bogeys") during tournament play, he had embraced a conservative strategy that was impeding his results.

Our solution wasn't to adopt a more aggressive strategy with his short irons. First, we needed to improve his chipping and pitching. Doing so would eliminate his justified fear of the "stupid bogey," thus freeing him up to take on a pin when it made sense to do so. The end result would be a shorter "Average Distance of Birdie Putt" which would result in a greater number of birdie putts made.

Making data-based decisions is as important in golf as it is in business. However, in both worlds, the data is not the answer—the answer is all in the interpretation!

noted that although Woods was No. 1 in the world, he still had a tendency to hit his drives out of play at inopportune times. From Nicklaus' point of view, an error like that was unacceptable and needed to be fixed, even if it meant finding a new teacher. That's how champions become champions: not only by dominating the outcomes (in this case, being the No. 1 golfer in the world) but also by mastering the contributing drivers of those outcomes.

CASE STUDY: MEASURING WHERE YOU STAND IN THE WORLD OF FINANCIAL ADVISING

Tracking performance stats, establishing benchmarks, and prioritizing critical drivers can be applied to any business where results matter. Here's an example, based on my work with financial advisors.

Financial advisors are accountable first and foremost for the dollars of production that they bring to their firms. An advisor's production is linked directly to the quantity of assets that he or she manages. So, from an outcomes point of view, success is dictated by amount of assets he or she can efficiently acquire and manage over time. The chart on page 97 is a sample outcome chart for an advisor.

The chart displays the advisor's performance versus an established benchmark, in this case the performance of a random sample of advisors within a defined region. The data below the chart show the outcomes of the advisor and those of advisors at the 50TH and 75TH percentile of the benchmark. The bar charts (above each set of data) display the percentile within which the advisor's data fall relative to the benchmark. Higher bars show strengths, while lower bars show weaknesses.

As you can quickly see from the chart, this advisor appears to be weak in the areas of net new assets and production per client.

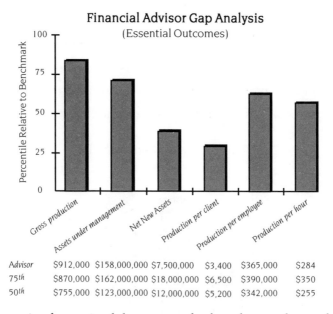

	Gross production	Assets under management	Net New Assets	Production per client	Production per employee	Production per hour
Advisor	$912,000	$158,000,000	$7,500,000	$3,400	$365,000	$284
75th	$870,000	$162,000,000	$18,000,000	$6,500	$390,000	$350
50th	$755,000	$123,000,000	$12,000,000	$5,200	$342,000	$255

Once we've determined that, we can look at the next layer of data to answer the question, "Why?"

The chart below shows that the advisor is obviously landing a high number of new clients, but the "average assets per new client" bar is very low.

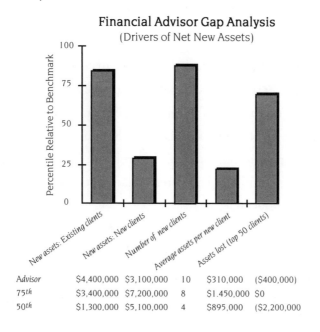

	New assets: Existing clients	New assets: New clients	Number of new clients	Average assets per new client	Assets lost (top 50 clients)
Advisor	$4,400,000	$3,100,000	10	$310,000	($400,000)
75th	$3,400,000	$7,200,000	8	$1.450,000	$0
50th	$1,300,000	$5,100,000	4	$895,000	($2,200,000)

Further investigation, using the chart below, shows that the "average assets per new referral" (meaning the average received from each new client obtained via referral) bar is also low, so the fact that this advisor is bringing in clients with relatively small amounts of assets appears to be tied to the kind of referrals he or she is getting.

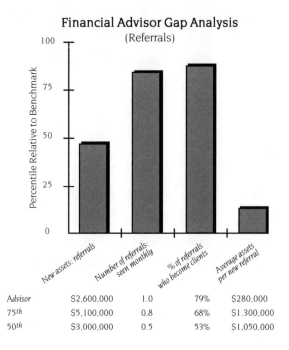

Financial Advisor Gap Analysis
(Referrals)

	New assets: referrals	Number of referrals: seen monthly	% of referrals who become clients	Average assets per new referral
Advisor	$2,600,000	1.0	79%	$280,000
75th	$5,100,000	0.8	68%	$1.300,000
50th	$3,000,000	0.5	53%	$1,050,000

Consider how important such data can be in creating a strategic plan that will target the factors that are driving the advisor's results. Without such data, the advisor might pursue training in sales skills or in generating additional referrals, even though neither of those areas would address the real cause of the problem. The data suggest that the advisor should build a strategic plan that will increase the average size of a referral.

With good information, the advisor can begin to ask the right question: How can I obtain more high-net-worth referrals? Measuring where you stand is a prerequisite to establishing targeted strategic plans in business. How might you use similar data in your business to track performance stats, establish benchmarks, and prioritize critical drivers?

SO WHERE DO YOU STAND?

Now let's take this concept a bit further into the realm of your business, whatever it might be. You'll remember the five factors that drive results we introduced in the last chapter. We referred to them as S.P.E.R.T.S. (skills, processes, experience, resources, tools, and strategies). Go back to the lists you made as part of the S.P.E.R.T.S. exercises in the previous chapter and select what you consider to be the three most essential of all the drivers you listed.

Which three of your drivers would best correlate with results in your business? Don't worry at this point whether you are weak or strong on any of the drivers. Simply decide which ones are most essential based on the impact you believe they'd have on your desired result if you were to be the best in your business at them. The three drivers you pick may come from three different categories or they may come from the same category.

Critical Driver #1: _____

Critical Driver #2: _____

Critical Driver #3: _____

For the above three drivers, ask yourself these questions:

1. *How would I quantify my level of performance for each of these drivers?*

2. *Who would be the most appropriate person for me to use as a benchmark at this point in my career?*

3. *How could I obtain my benchmark's performance stats for each driver so that I might measure where I stand?*

Use the worksheet below (or a separate sheet of paper) to jot down your ideas for each of the three questions above:

Best Measurement

1. _____

2. _____

3. _____

Appropriate Benchmarks

1. _____

2. _____

3. _____

Benchmark's Measurement

1. _____

2. _____

3. _____

I realize that not all businesses are as numbers-obsessed as golf and financial services are, but see what you can do. As an example, let's say you work in the world of retail and you wrote down "product knowledge" for Critical Driver No. 1 above. Whether you were a buyer or a salesperson in retail, your level of product knowledge (although difficult to measure in any quantifiable way) could have a significant impact on your results. But just because something is difficult to measure doesn't mean that we should forgo the process of measuring where we stand. Let's take a crack at it.

First, we might measure product knowledge by asking a sales manager or supervisor, whose experience and judgment we respect, to quiz us on the particulars of the products we represent. For more established businesses, written quizzes on product knowledge exist, but for most, the key questions reside between the ears of those with experience.

So if you sat for an hour and had the manager ask you a range of product-related questions, you could then have him or her measure where you stand relative to an agreed-upon benchmark, such as other individuals in similar roles, top salespeople in the company, buyers in other regions, etc. The answer might be expressed in terms of a one-to-100 scale, with 100 representing the best.

You could then ask the manager whether there are any obvious causes for your gaps in product knowledge, whatever they may be. For example, do you need to better understand how the product works, how it is made, or what customized versions are available for customers with more specialized needs?

The answers to these kinds of questions set the stage for you to train like a champion. As with all of the exercises in this book, try to be as candid with yourself as possible. This is your book and unless you choose to share it with others, nobody else needs to know what skills you plan to work on or how you plan to go about improving. Just let them marvel when they see the results!

CHAPTER 5

TRAIN LIKE A CHAMPION

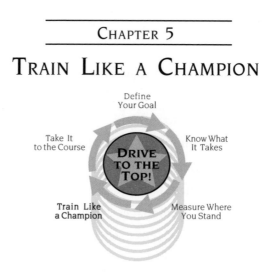

IF YOU REALLY WANT TO BE THE BEST IN YOUR BUSINESS, your next step is to train like a champion. Simply put, that means that you must:

1. Apply the three steps to mastery.
2. Surround yourself with winners.
3. Commit the time to train.
4. Tailor your training plan to your most essential needs.

In this chapter, we'll look at each one of these tactics in turn. Before reading on, though, take a quick moment to complete the following self-assessment. Like the exercises in the preceding chapters, it should help you better understand the points that follow and which ones may be most relevant to you.

Please read these statements and consider how descriptive each one is of you. Using a one-to-five scale (five being very descriptive, and one being not very descriptive) rate each item as it applies to you.

_____ 1. I know how to effectively develop a skill from the point of understanding what I have to do to actually doing it on the job.

_____ 2. I meet often with people who directly contribute to my professional development.

_____ 3. I set aside regular time in my schedule to improve my business knowledge and skills.

_____ 4. I pursue training that specifically addresses the things that keep me from performing at a higher level in my business.

_____ 5. I pursue opportunities for observation, supervision, and feedback from others about how I can further develop and implement my skills on the job.

_____ 6. I limit the time that I spend with people who bring me down, sap my positive energy, or distract me from what I need to do to succeed.

_____ 7. I can name specific training activities that I have engaged in over the past month that have improved my business effectiveness.

_____ 8. I show up to work each week with a plan of what I need to do to continually improve my productivity and effectiveness.

Take note of the items above that you ranked with a three or less. As you read on, consider what specific changes you can make in your behavior to increase your ability to train like a champion.

By "train like a champion," I mean something different from what many businesses think of as training. Though they may spend enormous sums on training programs, the results are often far from what they had hoped to achieve going in. Why is their training so often ineffective?

Several years ago I was brought in to work on a sales improvement initiative for a major retailer that was losing market share to its competitors. The company had done a good job of identifying the essential drivers of its sales (such as brand recognition, customer flow into stores, percentage of customers making purchases, average spending per customer, and so forth).

The company's data suggested that its marketing and branding initiatives were serving their purpose by bringing large numbers of customers through the door. However, there weren't enough shopping bags full of sold merchandise going back out the door.

Naturally, we wondered what exactly was going on inside the store that led to such poor sales. We decided to look more closely at how the salespeople were interacting with their customers.

The retailer's managers assured us that they had an established, well-defined effective sales process. However, having a process and making sure it's implemented are two very different things. We asked them, "How do you know that your salespeople are following the process?" The managers' responded, "Because they've all been trained."

Now, we've all attended training sessions in our careers, but how much of that training have we actually seen implemented? Again, receiving training and executing on that training are not the same thing.

After dispatching so-called "mystery shoppers" to the company's stores across the country, we discovered that most salespeople were not following the process at all. They had been trained on it, and they could even explain it when asked. They just weren't doing it.

As we probed further, we found several reasons for that. Among them were that salespeople didn't take the process seriously and managers weren't providing any sort of ongoing feedback to help them. What's more, there was no link between sales and compensation, giving salespeople little incentive to improve their performance.

The point here is that just because people know what to do doesn't mean they'll do it. The goal of effective training is to turn a skill, like retail selling, into a repeatable habit. Before that can happen, however, a person must master that skill. Mastery isn't the result of a single training session, or even a hundred of them. Mastery is a process, one that top athletes come to understand instinctively and that anyone in business can learn too.

Training Tactic #1: Apply the three steps to mastery.

For any training program to be truly effective, it should incorporate what I think of as the three steps to mastery: (1) Understanding, (2) Supervised practice, and (3) Transfer. I know of no better way to develop your skills to a point where you can apply them repeatedly and effectively under real-life conditions than by following these three steps of development. Here's an easy way to visualize the process:

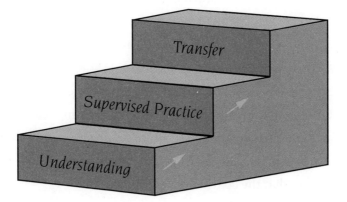

Unfortunately, far too many business-training initiatives that start at Step 1, Understanding, also stop there, as well. The trainer simply gathers people in a room and, at best, increases their understanding of what they ought to be doing. That kind of an educational/

knowledge-sharing session is a necessary step in changing behavior and adopting new skills, but it is only a first step.

In golf and other professional sports, on the other hand, this step is always followed by supervised practice, whether that's on the driving range, the ball field, the basketball court, or the ice. Great athletes enjoy the process of escorting a skill away from the understanding step and up onto the other two required steps to learning. In a conversation I had with four-time Major-champion, Meg Mallon, about her early experiences with the learning process, she said, "I loved to practice. It was never something that I considered hard. It was the work I looked forward to, and I enjoyed doing because I saw myself get better. I could go get a lesson [from coach Mike McGetrick] for an hour, and I'd actually spend the next three to five hours completely by myself just learning. They had those three practice holes back there, and I'd go by myself and beat balls and hit all kinds of shots. And that was to me and still is my favorite part about getting better—about competing and learning how to win."

> JUST BECAUSE PEOPLE KNOW WHAT TO DO DOESN'T MEAN THEY'LL DO IT.

Supervised practice helps athletes progress from simply understanding what they need to do to demonstrating that they can actually do it. During supervised practice, coaches work directly with athletes to make sure that they can implement the plays, skills, and strategies that the coaches have taught them.

In the business world, employees may leave a training session with a better understanding of a sales process, customer service philosophy, strategic plan, key account initiative, or whatever they're being taught. But whether they can actually execute on it, or even attempt to, is left to chance.

Photo by Darren Carroll, *Sports Illustrated*

"I loved to practice. . . . I could go get a lesson for an hour, and I'd actually spend the next three to five hours completely by myself just learning." —*Meg Mallon*

Smart businesses take their training initiatives a step farther, moving on to Step 2, Supervised Practice. They create hands-on exercises, partnering opportunities, and/or on-the-job coaching to provide that supervised practice.

In sports, these training sessions go beyond practicing skills in a static, sterile environment and take it to a still higher level. NBA coaches, for example, recognize that shooting free throws under ideal conditions in practice is quite different from doing it under game conditions. So what do they do? They use sound systems to pump fan noise into the practice sessions and exhaust their players with suicide sprints and game simulation drills. Then they require them to make a certain percentage of free throws before heading to the showers. In sports, we call this third step "transfer training," exposing athletes to the demands of competition during practice in order to push the transferability of skills.

When I was discussing training with the tennis great Ivan Lendl once, he told me he felt he had to take a skill through a series of stages in order to truly master it. Lendl said, "Step 1—You have to identify and decide how you are going to go about it. Step 2—You have to do it in practice. Step 3—You have to do it in a match. Step 4—You have to do it in a match under pressure, meaning four-all break point in the final set. And Step 5—You have to do it in a big match under pressure, meaning five-all in the fifth set tiebreaker at the U.S. Open finals."

In business, the notion of transferring a newly learned skill to a real-life situation is all too often little more than wishful thinking. The assumption—and it's a big assumption—is that the freshly trained employee will leave the training session, return to work, and automatically apply those new skills. More often than not, though, the employee never even attempts to do that. Why? For a whole bunch of reasons, including a greater level of comfort with doing things the old way, a fear of failure, lack of confidence, or simply having no incentive to take the risk of doing things differently.

Some of that fear on the part of newly trained employees is well justified. Without the benefit of a supervised training environment in which to transfer their skills, they have to attempt it themselves in the field—where, yes, the customer becomes the guinea pig. Customers are frequently unknowing participants in the transfer laboratory, and while they may not know exactly what's going on, they may know that they don't like it.

I'm not suggesting that a skill has to be flawlessly mastered before being field exposed. That wouldn't be practical or cost-effective. But we do have to recognize that there are tools we can use in business to accelerate the transfer of a skill, including on-the-job coaching, video and audiotape monitoring, the use of mystery shoppers to evaluate the sales process, and so forth. The bottom line is that we can't assume that just because a person has read a training manual or sat through a PowerPoint presentation that he or she will eventually master a particular skill. Mastery is a three-step process, and skipping any one of the steps can mean failure.

Training Tactic #2: Surround yourself with winners.

You can't underestimate the value of associating with other winners if you want to take your game to the next level. Or, for that matter, the damage you can do to your career by perpetually hanging out with people, who, for lack of a more polite term, we'll call losers.

Some time ago, I received a call from an NBA scout requesting that I consult with one of his team's recent drafts. The scout explained that the player had been recruited primarily because of his exceptional shooting ability, particularly from the 3-point range, and all involved were excited about the gains the team would derive

WHY "UNDERSTANDING" ISN'T ENOUGH

During the time you've played golf (for those of you who play), how many different swing errors have been pointed out to you? How many different fixes have you attempted? There seems to be no end to the information available to help us play better golf.

Has this increased understanding really made you better? For some, I'm sure it has. For others, the information overload has only created confusion and minimal long-term improvement at best.

During the past 20 years, I've met with thousands of golfers and teaching professionals, and by far, the primary inhibitor to player improvement is the lack of supervised practice and transfer training. Not lack of knowledge, not lack of access to a quality teaching professional, and certainly not lack of well-made (and cleverly marketed) golf equipment.

In golf, supervised practice involves a player hitting numerous balls in an attempt to master a new technique while under supervision. It is the ideal follow-up to a golf lesson. Transfer training is the next step, during which a player tries to apply the new skill in conditions commonly experienced on the golf course such as various random placement of the ball, distractions, or pressure.

Rather than taking a series of golf lessons, it's better to take one golf lesson followed by a series of training sessions. That gives you time to work on your new technique while under the supervision of a teaching professional.

In business, the lesson is the same. Simply understanding a new concept, procedure, or strategy isn't enough. You have to apply it, ideally under the supervision of someone who can provide feedback and make sure it is moving you closer to reaching your goals.

from this top prospect. Unfortunately, the gains were never realized, and the scout was puzzled as to why the player's performance declined so much once he was in the NBA. Choking? Couldn't handle the expectations? Was there too much pressure, or was he uncomfortable on the big stage?

Following the recommendation of the scout, the player was glad to meet with me to discuss his situation. During our first meeting, I asked him, "Do you know why I was asked to meet with you?" He replied "I haven't been shooting very well, and Jim [let's call him] wants me to figure out what I need to do to improve it. I was recruited because of my talent as a 3-point shooter and now I'm just not performing up to my potential. I guess you are here to help me."

I explained that our first task would be to identify the true cause of his slump. "Do you have any ideas as to why your performance is not up to par?" I asked.

With assurance, he responded, "I think I know exactly why I'm not performing."

"Why?" I asked.

"Because I don't want to!" he exclaimed.

Amazed, I inquired "You don't want to?"

"That's right, I don't want to. You see, I hate this place! It's not at all what I expected from an NBA team. I had better training and better coaching when I was in college. I come here and they do little more than provide you with a locker, some balls, and a gym. The coaching is mediocre at best. You see, I thrive on getting better, and while in school, each time I progressed to the next level, I loved that I received better and better training. I fully expected it would continue when I made it to the NBA. But, that wasn't the case, not here. It's terrible. So I need to get out of here, and the sure way out is to not perform."

Top athletes, top performers in all fields, are constantly on the lookout for people who can contribute in one way or another to their long-term achievements—coaches, fitness trainers, sports psychologists, nutritionists, agents, attorneys, accountants, and all the rest. They are especially eager to spend time with and seek insights from people who have already accomplished the things they yearn to achieve in their own careers.

In my particular line of work, I have practically become a stalker when it comes to top performers. And I am far from alone.

In a team sport like football, associating with winners often means getting on the right team. Consider seven-time all pro NFL cornerback Deion Sanders. Sanders played for the Atlanta Falcons from 1991 to 1994, and although he was considered one of the best defensive backs in the league, his team never won a Super Bowl while he was there. When he became a free agent, Deion Sanders made it a priority to shop around for a team that could win a Super Bowl. He wanted to surround himself with winners, and it worked. Before the end of his career, he had played on two Super Bowl championship teams, in San Francisco and in Dallas.

In an individual sport like golf, you can see the same principle at work. Top performers seek out other top performers. Tiger Woods, even as a mere rookie, set his sights on associating with winners like Mark O'Meara and Butch Harmon—champions in their own right. Jack Nicklaus, as a child, sought guidance from the likes of Bobby Jones and Jack Grout. Such golf greats could provide Woods and Nicklaus with advice on everything: how to handle the media, approach the Majors, and even how much to tip the locker room attendants.

Furthermore, champions like Tiger Woods and Jack Nicklaus take it in their own hands to initiate such mentoring relationships. You can bet that winners like O'Meara and Jones aren't looking for rookie golfers to hang out with and dispense advice to. But surprisingly, these legends are often more than happy to share their expertise, their experiences, and their insights—yes, even with rookies.

By contrast, who do you think most of the other rookies are hanging out with at tournaments, while the rare few like Tiger Woods are pursuing winners? Most rookies on tour hang out with other rookies because that's what makes them comfortable. Those are their friends, guys their age and more or less at their own level of accomplishment. There's nothing wrong with doing that, but it's not going to get you where you want to be anytime soon.

I have to actively push clients of mine to seek out people who can be of help in getting them to that next level. Why? Because, most of us don't want to impose on other people. We know how valuable our time is and we may assume that theirs is even more valuable.

But do you know what? If you ask, you may be surprised at just how willing many such men and women are to help. Not all of them, certainly, but a surprisingly high percentage. Why? Because in almost every case they have been there themselves. Every successful person in any field you can name was once a rookie, looking up to the greats of their day. Now that they have become the greats of their own time, they are, in many cases, more than happy to assist someone they perceive as a potential winner. For them it may be an ego booster. For you, it can be a priceless source of advice.

I remember the conversation I had with Jack Nicklaus in 2002, just after Tiger Woods split from his long-time coach Butch Harmon. Interestingly, Nicklaus told me, "I'd be more than happy to help [Tiger]. He just hasn't asked me." A further demonstration of how willing the champions of one generation often are to help out those of the next.

In business, men and women who are determined to succeed also look for other winners who can help them reach that next level. Howard

Schultz, the entrepreneur who turned the Starbucks Coffee Company into the juggernaut of java, was still seeking mentors even after he had become a success by any measure. In his autobiography, *Pour Your Heart Into It*, he writes, "To any entrepreneur, I would offer this advice: Once you've figured out what you want to do, find someone who has done it before." A bit later, he adds, "And with the right mentor, don't be afraid to expose your vulnerabilities. Admit you don't know what you don't know. When you acknowledge your weaknesses and ask for advice, you'll be surprised how much others will help."

Let me also give you an example from my own experience. When I was in graduate school, studying to be a sports psychologist, I had some really terrific, supportive professors. But none of them had done the sort of work I dreamed of doing with professional golfers. However, I learned that a man named Dr. Bob Rotella, director of sports psychology at the University of Virginia, was consulting with PGA and LPGA professionals with great success. I got Dr. Bob's phone number, and with a little trepidation, I called him from my home in Gainesville, Florida. I asked him if I could come up and have lunch with him.

Now, Dr. Bob didn't know me, and there wasn't much that I, just a graduate student, could do to benefit someone of his stature. Frankly, I wouldn't have blamed him if he'd said he was just too busy to take the time. But he agreed to see me anyhow. For me, it was a 12-hour car ride up to Charlottesville for a one-hour lunch. But it was time well spent. Dr. Bob was accommodating, inspirational, and insightful. He directed me toward coursework he thought would be useful for me, suggested how I might gain much-needed experience, and, most importantly, made my dream seem much more reachable. That one hour made a huge difference in my life.

So, ask yourself who are your Butch Harmons, your Jack Grouts, and your Dr. Bobs. They don't have to be famous. In fact, most probably won't be, although they may be well known and respected among their peers. Are these people in your company, or your industry? Or are they top performers in other fields with whom you feel a particular affinity? Write their names down in the spaces below, or use a separate sheet of paper if you wish. Once you've listed five, rank order them from (1) most likely to be influential in helping you reach your goal to (5) least influential. Next, rank them from (1) most accessible to you to (5) least accessible.

My Winners	Influence Rank	Accessibility Rank
1. _____	_____	_____
2. _____	_____	_____
3. _____	_____	_____
4. _____	_____	_____
5. _____	_____	_____

Which of the people on your list have both a high influence and high accessibility ranking? What can you do to arrange some time with them? If you don't already know them, or have some connection to them, is there someone else you know who can offer an introduction? Maybe your goal is a lunch or some other face-to-face situation. Perhaps it's a phone call or simply an exchange of e-mails. Even a now-and-then phone or e-mail relationship with someone who could be of help to you can pay enormous dividends in moving you to that next level. You may, in time, have an entire network of such people with particular strengths in the different areas you have decided to work on.

Also ask yourself, who do you spend your free time with? Who are the people you go to lunch with, hang out with around the water cooler, or go out for a drink with after work? Are they other winners who can help spur you on to greater achievement or people who may simply be holding you back? If you feel like it, make a list of people you'd prefer to spend less time with, those energy-sappers. Or just keep that second list in your head for future reference.

There is nothing wrong with people who lack your ambition or drive to succeed. They can be good, loyal friends and enrich your life in many ways. Not everybody can be a champion in life or even wants to be one.

On the other hand, people who sap your energy by virtue of their own negativity or who, worse still, belittle your desire to achieve, are an impediment to your success and should be given as little opportunity as possible to inflict their damage.

Now back to that list of winners that you generated earlier. As a first step, select one person from the list, and write his or her name and phone number in the spaces below. It's okay to put down this book and locate that phone number. Jot down the activity that you'd want to suggest (such as a lunch, phone call, observing that person on the job, or whatever). Now, write the date of one week from today next to it. That is your outside deadline for making the connection. No procrastinating beyond that point.

If you're reluctant to try, tell yourself that this one contact may change the direction of your life forever! And the next one after this (and the one after that) will be easier.

My Winning Contact: Phone number:

_____   _____

Intended activity: Date by which to contact:

_____   _____

HIRING OTHER WINNERS

If you are in management (or hope to be), you probably understand the importance of surrounding yourself with winners. Although this chapter is focused on training, I'm a firm believer in hiring winners who value training.

In team sports, coaches go to great lengths (and incredible expense) to ensure that they hire winners. Taking a closer look at the hiring process used in professional sports can provide valuable insights into how to hire in a business setting.

Picture yourself picking up your daily newspaper, turning to the job ads and reading:

"WANTED: WIDE-RECEIVER FOR NFL TEAM. FOUR YEARS COLLEGIATE FOOTBALL EXPERIENCE REQUIRED. PLEASE FAX RÉSUMÉ, REFERENCES, AND THREE LETTERS OF RECOMMENDATION TO . . ."

Can you imagine? It's unthinkable, right? Yet, we see it done every day in business.

Sports teams would never use a hiring process like that to fill their rosters. Why? Because it would not produce the best results, and achieving results is the ultimate goal, not simply filling a position.

So what do top franchises do instead? They define their needs in terms of specific competencies, scout collegiate players and free agents for the best fit, assess prospects via observation and testing, and then target, draft, and recruit winners.

Is there any reason why, in business, we should not be doing the same thing?

Training Tactic #3: **Commit the time to train.**

In the world of professional sports, athletes carve out time for training on a regular basis. For them, training is not an option but an absolutely essential and regular activity.

Although they spend a fair amount of time competing, athletes and their coaches devote even more hours to preparing for competition. In a study of NBA basketball coaches, for example, researchers found that the coaches spent four hours of preparation time for every hour of on-court time. By the same token, touring golf professionals literally hit hundreds of balls in practice for every single ball they hit in tournament play.

Tiger Woods' former coach, Butch Harmon, said that Woods was the hardest worker he'd ever known—and he'd also coached Greg Norman, who would hit balls each day until "he couldn't see anymore."

I once asked Harmon to describe a typical training day with Woods, and he recalled, "Tiger would be at the golf school at eight o'clock in the morning, and he had already been in the gym since five. He would hit balls for about an hour, go into the studio and we would look at it all on film and talk about some different positions. . . . He would go back and hit some more balls, then he went into the short-game area and he would stay there all day. He stayed down there for about five hours hitting wedge and pitch shots."

For many of us, a routine like that can be exhausting merely to read about. For a champion like Woods, it is exhilarating. And the results speak for themselves.

In the world of business, men and women often become so busy simply doing their jobs that they don't commit the time for training and professional development. True, the work may get done, but the results are almost sure to fall short of what we are capable of delivering. And we accomplish very little in the way of personal improvement in the long run. Worse still, we may also burn out more quickly.

Beginning golfers often tell me, "I just can't find the time to practice." My answer is this: *Finding* time doesn't work, you have to *make* time. Time is the ultimate measure of your priorities, your choices, and your commitments. If you want to be a good golfer, you must commit time to train for your game. If you want to succeed in business, you must commit time to train for the game of business. Starbucks' chairman, Howard Schultz, steadfastly attributes his company's success to its commitment to training, saying "In fact, we spend more money on training than we do on advertising. . . . We have no secret sauce, whatsoever. The only competitive advantage we have is the relationship we've built with our people and the relationships they have built with the customer."

> **FINDING** TIME DOESN'T WORK, YOU HAVE TO **MAKE** TIME.

Believe me; I know personally how difficult making the time for training can be. In business, as in sports, we rarely have the luxury of taking time off to train. We're doing our training at the same time we're out there competing. We have to go to work every day and at the same time find those spare moments during the week to develop our skills. Athletes are doing exactly the same thing. They're competing each week but at the same time trying to build time into their schedules to raise their skill set. To them it's training time plus tournament time. Whatever the name, it's a challenge we all face.

My first job out of college was as a staff psychologist at the counseling center at the University of Florida. In that role I provided counseling, training, and consulting services to university students and departments. Our counseling center had a seemingly endless supply of "customers" needing our services, and the waiting list seemed to stretch to infinity. Fortunately my boss recognized the need for the staff to continually develop our skills in addition to servicing our customers on a day-to-day basis. So, we set four hours out of every 40-hour week aside for professional development time; a full 10 percent of our working hours.

To some, this may have seemed like an extravagance, but my experience was that it was beneficial both to the staff and to our clients. We had the opportunity to develop professionally, and the quality and efficiency of the care we were able to deliver improved as well. Had our only goal been to chip away at that waiting list, we could have spent every waking hour in "service mode." Meanwhile, our professional development would have had to wait for another day; one that would never come.

I don't have to tell you that in our "get it done yesterday" world, time is one of the most valuable commodities you have and that deploying it effectively is critical to getting where you want to be.

How you choose to spend your working hours can determine whether you meet your deadlines, beat competitors to the punch, provide cost-effective services for your clients, or have the time to pursue the training that you need to keep improving your skills and moving ever upward.

Are you working in an environment that allows time for you to continue to develop professionally, or are you on the non-stop hamster wheel of service? My early job experience taught me to structure my own work to build in time for professional development, no matter how busy I was with my everyday responsibilities. Anyone can benefit from having that kind of opportunity.

Do you commit the time to train on a regular basis? Do you attend training sessions, read relevant books, or shadow top performers in your industry? Take a moment and reflect on your answers to the following three questions:

1.   *What training have you completed over the past year that specifically addresses one of the greatest gaps among your performance drivers (the S.P.E.R.T.S. we discussed in Chapter 3)?*

_____

_____

_____

2.   *How could you ensure that you are spending more energy than your competitors (including friendly competitors within your own organization) on improving your skills?*

_____

_____

_____

3.   *What specific activities do you have planned in the next three months to improve in areas that have a direct impact on your business results?*

_____

_____

_____

Training Tactic #4: Tailor your training plan to your most essential needs.

Businesspeople often gripe about having to attend training sessions. And no wonder. Very likely, they have been subjected over the years to faddish training programs that did very little to improve their real-world performance. The training was probably provided

ARE YOU PLAYING AN INDIVIDUAL OR TEAM SPORT?

In individual sports like golf, players must master all the essential skills that correlate with results: ball-striking, putting, and short-game. If there's a weak spot in any of those, it will show in a player's score.

In team sports like football, athletes are position players. Each must master a subset of roles required for team success: kickers kick, linemen block, receivers catch, and so forth. No one expects every player to do it all. Coaches in team sports don't even try to create an all-position player. Instead, they build on the strengths of separate position players.

Depending on the business you're in, you may be playing either an individual or a team "sport."

Does your job require you to master a wide range of skills? It might, for example, if you run a small office or own a business. You may be making a sales call one hour, fixing the photocopier an hour later, and then balancing the books after that. In that case, your work more closely resembles an individual sport.

By contrast, can you hand off a weakness of yours to a fellow teammate who is better in that area and instead focus your time and energy on your strengths? Here your business more resembles the team model. This is likely to be the case if you work for a large organization. Your job may be to make sales calls, fix photocopiers, or balance the books, but probably not all three.

Your goal should be to approach your work in a way that's consistent with the "type of sport" you are playing, team or individual, and to seek training opportunities that will help you advance along whichever career path you've chosen.

by presenters who didn't have the faintest idea of what their audience actually did for a living. What's more, the recipients of this force-fed training were probably never shown any direct relationship between training and results, or training and rewards; probably because there was no relationship.

As Intel co-founder Andrew Grove once observed, "It's very important for the heads of organizations to be focused on results, measuring results, rewarding results, and not conduct, behavior, styles, and all these other things that have, at best, a tenuous and speculative link to results."

Believe me; top athletes have even less patience when it comes to faddish nonsense that has no clear connection to improving their game. Hockey legend Bobby Orr summed it up this way, "Forget about style. Worry about results." For top athletes, every minute of training time is a precious opportunity, not to be squandered, and woe to anybody who tries to interfere with it.

Butch Harmon, Tiger Woods' former coach, once told me how Tiger approaches the driving range. "When he comes to the tee, he comes to practice with a plan, every day of his life. He just doesn't go to the range [thinking,] 'I'm going to hit balls.' He goes to the range with a plan. 'This is what I need to work on.' Great players want to improve, so on what they don't do well is what they spend most of their time practicing. But I think you have to specifically program that in for the day. You have to say, 'This is what I'm going to do; this is what I'm going to work on.' Then you go do it."

In other words, professional athletes, and top performers in every field, come to work with a plan, not only one for how to do their job, but also a plan for what they can do during the day to *improve* how they do their job.

In sports, the purpose of training is clear: to build knowledge, processes, and/or skills. Training is not the end; rather it is the means to an end. If it isn't producing the desired result, athletes and coaches will change it. In business, this message often gets lost.

As a presenter and trainer at a variety of national and regional conferences each year, I am frequently asked to participate in company training programs. Often I get a call from a manager, training director, or meeting planner who says something like, "We'd like to know if you're available to speak at our national sales meeting in Las Vegas in February?"

I say, "I'd be happy to. What would you like the presentation to focus on?"

Then they will often say, "What do you have?"

What do I have? I feel like a waiter in a restaurant, as if I should now reel off my list of "today's specials" until I hit a training program that sounds appetizing enough to order.

Well-intentioned as the callers may be, they are making what I consider a fundamental and all-too-common mistake. They see training as an end in and of itself. The goal in arranging for it seems to be simply to fill a particular time slot in the program, with little regard to the nature or ultimate intention of that training. The link between training and building essential skills has somehow been lost. Before long, in these situations, employees come to discount training as a meaningless exercise and all-around waste of time and money. And, all too often, they're exactly right.

Instead of "What do you have?" callers who truly understand the value of training will ask a more sophisticated kind of question. For example, "We're trying to sharpen our sales force's ability to identify, measure, and develop their most critical sales skills. Could you reinforce this process while relating it to your work with elite athletes?"

To train like a champion, you must first prioritize your performance drivers and begin to address the one or two that will

Photo by Mike Ehrmann, *Sports Illustrated*

"For me it just happens.
I just get out of my own way and let the training just take over." —*Tiger Woods*

have the greatest effect on your results. This kind of prioritization is done every day by top coaches who recognize that time is a finite commodity and there's none to waste on trial-and-error learning. They strive to identify the one or two areas with the most potential for a particular athlete and create a personalized training program that addresses them.

Unfortunately, too many amateur athletes spend the bulk of their time leveraging their strengths but ignoring and, in fact, exacerbating their weaknesses. This is the equivalent of perfectly rowing a leaking boat. You may improve your already excellent rowing technique, but meanwhile, the boat will be sinking under you. Men and women in business often have exactly the same problem.

Golf coach Butch Harmon was confident that one reason Tiger Woods rose to the top of the game was his ability to focus on the things he did not do well and then work on them. As Harmon put it to me, "The people we teach in our clubs only practice what they do well, because they don't want to do what they don't do well—because that's no fun. Great players…they want to improve, so what they don't do well is what they spend most of their time practicing."

Engaging in activities that allow you to leverage your strengths is certainly wise, particularly if you work within a team environment. Nevertheless, each of us have weaknesses that limit our ability to achieve our upper potential. We must seek training to eliminate these weaknesses.

When was the last time that you actively pursued training with the goal of eliminating an essential weakness or developing a new skill or process that was critical to your results? Whether you are managing a company's training initiatives or overseeing your own personal program, your training efforts should, whenever possible, be designed to meet your (or your organization's) most essential needs.

Dr. Rick Jensen 127

To get the most value from your limited training time, answer the following questions:

1.   *Reflect back on the three critical drivers that you identified in the previous chapter. If you could attend any training, organizational improvement, or coaching initiative, which of these drivers are most in need of such attention?*

_____

_____

_____

2.   *Where will you look for this training? (It might, for example, be available within your company or through a program sponsored by your industry trade association.) Who will you contact to get the ball rolling—and when? Set a deadline to make that call.*

_____

_____

_____

Before we finish this chapter, I want to let you in on a little secret. Even though I spend a lot of my time training top performers, I find the research on training to be pretty discouraging, because often, even the best training is not very productive.

Why is that? It's mainly because people don't act on it quickly enough. The research is pretty clear that the sooner you engage in the process of mastering something you've learned, the more likely it is to have a measurable impact on your performance. If there's a delay between your exposure to information and your initial implementation of it, whatever you've learned tends just to get filed away in your head somewhere, along with the rules of trigonometry and the names of the 50 state capitals.

Consider how many training programs you've attended where you've received a manual with outlines, PowerPoint slides, charts, graphs, and best practices. However, if you are like most people, those materials eventually found their way to the trash can or, at best, were shelved away to collect dust until a later date when you happen to be moving offices or making room for more training manuals.

The next time you receive a training manual at a conference or workshop, try something new. Before leaving the conference, turn to the back cover of the manual, and in big print, write the one or two actions that you will take immediately to gain benefit from your training. You'll still have all of your notes from the conference stored within your manual, but what's most important is that you prioritize and commit to several specific actions that you will implement immediately following the event. When you get back to your office, put the manual in a conspicuous place on your desk, not tucked away on a shelf, and leave it there until you've implemented your action items. When you've completed your actions, turn to the back cover again and jot down the number of days it took you to benefit from your training. Then (and only then) file the manual away, for later reference (or not!). Remember, all the training (or training literature) in the world isn't going to do you any good unless you apply it, and apply it right away.

We've discussed what I've called the three steps to mastery— from understanding, to supervised practice, and transfer. The ultimate goal of any mastery initiative is to create lifelong habits of success. True champions make the final leap by taking a skill from the training environment to the real world, where they apply it, own it, and live it. I call that "taking it to the course," and it's the subject of our next chapter.

GETTING FIT—AND STAYING THAT WAY

Greg Norman once told me, "I work out four to six days per week, two hours each day. You have to work out in this game today. If you don't, you won't be fit enough to hit the number of balls necessary to stay on top."

Professional athletes obviously need to stay fit. Less obvious, but becoming more evident all the time, is the role that fitness plays in business success. The more fit you are, the more likely that you will be able to manage the daily demands that are placed on your body and mind—and to keep up with the greater challenges you're likely to face as you achieve even higher levels of responsibility.

If you are already reasonably fit, you probably know it. Congratulations. Your challenge will be to stay that way. If you aren't fit, you also know that. Your job will be to get fit and then maintain that level of fitness. There's no shortage of good information available on fitness. What most of us lack, of course, is the self-discipline to master that information.

My advice to men and women who are serious about getting and staying fit is to pursue supervised practice with a trained fitness instructor for a period of time.

If your first response to this suggestion is to think, "I don't need a trainer. I can do it on my own," then ask yourself why you haven't.

Once you've established some sound exercise and eating habits under professional (or capable amateur) guidance, try to fly without a net, for a week at first, then two, and then more. You may fall once in a while. If so, pick yourself up and try again. If you need to, consult your instructor again, but for a shorter period of time. Then try going it alone once more. Stick with it until your new exercise and eating habits have become integral to your routine.

CHAPTER 6

TAKE IT TO THE COURSE

ONE AFTERNOON, I WAS HAVING LUNCH WITH BUTCH HARMON at Arnold Palmer's Bay Hill Club & Lodge in Orlando, Florida. I asked Butch , who was still coaching Tiger Woods at the time, what he thought separated Tiger from the other players on the PGA Tour. He quickly responded, "Tiger's willingness and ability to take it to the course." He further explained that Tiger, unlike other players, could take a skill that they were working on and apply it in tournament play much sooner than other players could.

In business, such skill is referred to as "execution" or "implementation"—in golf, pros refer to it as "taking it to the course." Butch explained that Tiger was willing to take the risk associated with trying something new even in a setting that could publicly expose that he had yet to *own* the new skill. This was because of Tiger's desire to "push the transfer" of a skill.

The ultimate goal of any improvement initiative is to benefit from the result you hope to achieve. So why not push the transfer of the initiative as quickly as possible? Yes, there may be some setbacks, failures, or even public criticism associated with the effort. But the sooner the transfer occurs, the sooner the benefit is likely to happen.

In 1998, Butch and Tiger were highly scrutinized for making significant changes to Tiger's golf swing. Why would you ever change something that has proven to be so effective? Woods was, if you recall, ranked the No. 1 player on the PGA Tour money list in 1997.

Champions want to get better—always! Even when they are No. 1 in the world, they pursue improvement initiatives and push the transfer of these initiatives with the knowledge that they may be criticized. Criticism, public scrutiny, and lack of guaranteed success are part of the process. However, resting on past accomplishments is not an option. In competitive environments, if you stand still, you will soon be passed by. You must continue to develop your capabilities and take them to the course as soon as possible.

Interestingly, in 2007, Tiger made a valiant run at Byron Nelson's record of 11 consecutive PGA Tour wins. Tiger ran off a streak of seven consecutive wins on the PGA Tour—and he did so after again being highly scrutinized for changing his swing with his coach, Hank Haney. Woods lost that eighth tournament, but nobody will be surprised when he takes another run at the record. For champions, the pursuit of excellence never ends.

Do you, like Tiger Woods, have the will and ability to take it to the course? In this chapter, we will discuss the strategies and mindset that champions use to take it to the course. First, however, take a moment to complete the following self-assessment.

Using a one-to-five scale (five being very descriptive, and one being not very descriptive) rate each item as it applies to you.

_____ 1. I do not let fear of failure, criticism, or public scrutiny keep me from pursuing initiatives that could improve my results.

_____ 2. I take the necessary steps to turn best practices into routines that are consistent, repeatable, and part of my regular business procedures.

_____ 3. I am not a procrastinator. If I think something will help my business results, I act on it immediately.

_____ 4. I hold myself (and others when appropriate) accountable for implementing the plans I set to improve my business performance.

_____ 5. I rely on a positive mental attitude to cope with the time and energy expenditure that accompanies a significant change.

_____ 6. Others see me as disciplined, organized, and systematic in my approach to implementing procedures and strategies that will make a difference in my business results.

_____ 7. I am not inclined to "paralysis by analysis." Once I decide on a course of action, I put the pedal to the metal and execute it.

_____ 8. I monitor performance measures that indicate whether or not my training efforts are accomplishing the intended result.

Take note of the items above that you ranked with a three or less. As you read on, consider what you might do differently to increase your ability to "take it to the course."

Once you have committed to some of the principles we've talked about earlier in this book, I know you'll begin to see improvement in your ability to perform. But as we discussed in our review of the three steps to mastery in the last chapter, you must push knowledge and skill up onto the third step, transfer, in order to reap the benefits of your training. Think of this third step as "taking it to the course." This is where the rubber meets the road, where we truly see the impact of our efforts. "Taking it to the course" is so important that it is worthy of its own chapter.

One thing about world-class athletes that has always impressed me is that once they learn something that may be useful, they apply it. Most people aren't like that. Have you ever said that you wanted to do something like lose weight or get in shape? Have you even bought a book or watched a tape to help you do it? And did it work? If you're like most people, it probably didn't.

I would argue that most of the diet industry (the endless flood of books, tapes, magazine articles, classes, and everything else) is designed to provide consumers with knowledge on how to lose weight. However, lack of knowledge is not the problem; more often than not, it's that we just don't apply the knowledge. We know we should eat better, but we don't. We know we should work harder to get in shape, but we don't.

We all know lots of things. The problem is, we often don't take the next step and execute on them. Top athletes, as I said, are different. A top golfer will have a discussion with another player or listen to a coach, and say, "I think that's a good idea for me, I'm going to do it." And that's exactly what happens.

Touring golf pros often make swing improvements during practice that to their surprise do not hold up under the pressure of competition. The reason is that the newly changed skills, developed in a practice environment, have yet to be put to the test under playing conditions. Taking these new skills to the course and learning how they will function under the pressures of competition is the necessary and final step in making a change that will show real results.

Similarly, in business, reading a book or attending a training session meant to improve a set of skills or introduce a new business process will not have an immediate impact on your business performance. Establishing how and when you will transition this new knowledge into your work is the essential next step.

The late W. Clement Stone, Chicago insurance magnate and author of several popular self-help books, including *Success through a Positive Mental Attitude*, suggested using a procedure he called "R2A2." Though that may sound like the name of a lesser-known Star Wars robot, it's actually a shrewd analysis of the steps by which we can wring the most benefit of any new knowledge. The R2 part stands for *recognizing* the value of the new information and then *relating* it to your own situation. The A2 stands for *assimilating* the information and *applying* it in real life; in other words taking it to the course.

To effectively take any new knowledge to the course, you must make sure that you:

1.   Embrace the mindset of a champion
2.   Turn best practices into routines
3.   Take action NOW
4.   Establish accountability for results

Let's look at these, step by step.

Step #1: Embrace the mindset of a champion

In tournament play, professional golfers rely on a mindset that supports the transfer of their skills to the competitive arena. Pros recognize that their mental approach to the game can have a significant impact on whether their skills show up when they most need them.

In business we must also manage our mindset in order to maximize our potential and excel in the constantly changing competitive landscape. Here are three mental toughness strategies that will help you embrace the mindset of a champion, followed by a complete explanation of each:

- Learn from Failure
- Thrive on Adversity
- Play the Game

Learn from Failure

Come game time, one particular mental challenge that confronts all golfers and other athletes who pursue excellence is the possibility of failure. How they perceive and respond to the possibility of failure—and, indeed, to failure itself—can significantly affect their ability to transfer new skills.

In golf, failure may be experienced at a number of different levels; losing a match, missing a cut, hitting a ball out of bounds, missing a three-foot putt, or playing above one's handicap. In the game of golf, players often fall short of their desired goal.

In business, we experience failure in very similar ways. We present business proposals that get rejected, we lose new accounts to our competitors, we have key clients that start doing business elsewhere, and we even miss our sales goals from time to time. Failure comes with the territory, whether you compete in sports or business.

People who do not see failure for what it is may find the competitive arena very frustrating. Until they acknowledge that failure is an unavoidable, inherent (and hopefully, infrequent) occurrence in all competitive endeavors, they will continue to deal with it through counterproductive means: making excuses, blaming someone else, rationalizing, berating themselves, and even avoiding competition altogether.

Photo by Bob Martin, *Sports Illustrated*

"I don't really look at it as failure. It's more of a learning process.
Failure is a part of success." —*Beth Daniel*

LPGA Hall of Fame inductee Beth Daniel once told me how she perceives and reacts to a blown opportunity, a missed cut, or a poor tournament. "I don't really look at it as failure. It's more of a learning process," she explained. "Failure is a part of success. The best way to learn is to fail."

What is critical isn't the failure but how you deal with it when it happens. As Vince Lombardi once said, "It's not whether you get knocked down; it's whether you get up." Top golfers have learned to face failure head-on and use their mental toughness to get back up after being knocked down. Touring pros

> FAILURE COMES WITH THE TERRITORY, WHETHER YOU COMPETE IN SPORTS OR BUSINESS.

do not fear failing or avoid situations where failure is likely; instead, they prepare themselves to minimize the chances of failure and then they push the limits of their talents on the golf course. When failure presents itself, top players cope with it, learn from it, and move on.

During the final round of the 2007 Open Championship at Carnoustie, Padraig Harrington stood on the 18th tee with a one-shot lead over Sergio Garcia, who was still on the golf course several groups behind him. Harrington made double-bogey on the hole, relinquishing the lead to Garcia. He walked off the green, picked up his son, smiled, and gave him a great big hug. He headed to the scorers' hut, signed his scorecard, and then he sat awaiting the consequences as Garcia played his last several holes.

Would his double-bogey cost him a chance at being the first Irishman since 1947 to win the Claret Jug? Would Sergio struggle on his final holes and give it back to Harrington? What about the possibility of a playoff? As Harrington waited for the answers to these questions, he later remembered, "I sat there in that hut, and I was as disciplined as I could be with my focus not to brood [about it]…I never let it cross my mind that I'd just thrown away the Open."

As it happened, the double-bogey on the final hole of regulation by Harrington did open the door for Garcia, who arrived on the 18th green facing a 10-footer for par to win his first major championship. Garcia lipped out the putt and made bogey, sending the Open Championship to a four-hole playoff, which Harrington won. Keeping failure in perspective can often lead to success!

Arnold Palmer was known for his willingness to attack a golf course. Is there any question that his approach would be accompanied by many failed opportunities?

Palmer once observed that, "Even when I have been playing at my worst, or when all the breaks have been going against me, I approach each new day, each new hole, as a glorious opportunity to get going again." Palmer's ability to look forward rather than dwell on past failures is a common quality of world class athletes. Chris Evert, one of the most accomplished tennis champions in history used a similar approach to dealing with failure. "I was consistent over a long period of time because I never looked back, never dwelled on my defeats," she said. "I always looked ahead."

Dealing with failure is a skill. Champions have developed that skill. You can, too. Recognize that failure is a part of the game. Embrace it, cope with it, learn from it, and move on.

Thrive on Adversity

I'd be kidding you if I said that whenever you "took it to the course," every single time you tried to win, you'd succeed. Life just doesn't work that way, at least for most of us.

But a champion faces even the inevitable setbacks differently. One time I was speaking at a sales conference where one of the

Photo by Tony Triolo, *Sports Illustrated*

"The first thing I do after losing. . .is to forget it.
I take a look at my calendar and start thinking about where we'll be playing
next week, and I'll show 'em then!" —*Nancy Lopez*

other speakers was Bill Russell, the great Boston Celtics center, NBA Hall of Fame inductee, five-time NBA most valuable player, and 12-time all-star. In other words, this guy knows a thing or two about winning.

During dinner I had a chance to talk with him, and I did what I always do when I have an opportunity to sit down with a great athlete. I picked his brain and asked him all kinds of things, like, "Why do you think you dominated so much in basketball? What was your key?"

He said, "My main key was creativity."

So naturally I asked him what he meant by creativity. And this is what he said (I wrote it down on a napkin): "I always believed that every player had one perfect game in him, so at the start of every game I always thought that tonight is going to be that perfect game. When it didn't happen, I went back to work and practiced to develop those skills that I thought kept it from happening. I was still learning in the last game that I ever played."

What he meant by "creativity" was that he had to adjust his strategy each and every game if he was ever going to achieve that perfect one. So every game he played he altered his previous strategy just a bit to see if that would make the difference. If something didn't work, he just figured he'd at least learned something and moved on to the next one.

Of course it's one of the biggest clichés in the world to write off a bad experience as a "learning opportunity." But there's also a lot of truth to it. And it's certainly more healthy psychologically and more productive on a purely practical level to couch it in those terms.

Psychologists sometimes refer to this as "positive reframing." For example, one of the things I'll do with athletes is to throw hypothetical situations at them. With golfers I'll say, "You had a great lead, but you blew it and now you're coming down to the last hole and you're tied. How are you going to think about that? Are you going to say, 'Here I am choking again?' Or, could you reframe it as something like, 'If on Thursday someone would have told me I'd be tied for the lead coming into the final hole, I'd be thrilled.' So enjoy the moment!

Here are some other examples:

Negative	Positive
"I don't deserve to win."	"Today could be my day."
"I'm not any good at this."	"I'm going to give it my best effort."
"Everyone is watching me."	"Let's see what I can do."

Remember, what's changing here isn't the reality of the situation, but how you choose to perceive the reality. If your ball's in a sand trap, for example, you can either say to yourself, "I know I'm going to blow this shot; I always do." Or you could tell yourself something like this, "Great, an opportunity to try out my new technique with my sand wedge." Your ball is in the same place, either way. That's the reality.

You want to reframe the situation because the way you perceive it can have a real effect on your performance. Thinking positively may not get you out of that sand trap in and of itself, but thinking negatively almost certainly won't.

The top golfers take it a step further. Not only do they refuse to let adversity get them down, but they actually seem to embrace it and thrive on it.

One of the reasons golf is such a challenging game is that adverse situations can arise during virtually every round. The adversity may be due to factors outside a player's control, like the weather, poor course conditions, or rude playing partners. Or it may be the result of mental or physical factors within a player's control. Almost without exception, a player is going to have to deal with some form of adversity during a round.

ALL BUSINESS HAS ITS UPS AND DOWNS

Have you ever wondered why players' golf scores can vary so much from one round to another? Some days they shoot 68, other days they shoot 76. These fluctuations in performance from day-to-day are normal, and no matter how much one tries, they will never be eliminated.

Most people attempt to explain away these expected day-to-day fluctuations in their performance, whether in sports or in business. Just sit around the 19th hole for a while and you will hear golfers attempting to explain away their scores. "I didn't putt very well today." Or, "I had two bad holes, otherwise I would have shot 72."

Eavesdrop on a weekly sales team meeting and you will hear salespeople doing the same. "The stock market has everyone scared to buy." Or, "I never received the new marketing materials."

While daily performance may be uncontrollable, you can and should attempt to control the variables that will influence your average performance over time. I refer to these variables as the three "critical success factors" - (1) Talent (2) Interference, and (3) Luck. The following formula shows how the three critical success factors will influence your performance on any given day:

PERFORMANCE = Talent – Interference +/- Luck

Talent, in the sense I'm using it here, is the sum total of your physical, strategic, cognitive, and technical efforts. Fortunately, your talent is something you have control over. It is the result of the quantity and quality of your training, as we previously discussed.

Interference means anything that detracts from your efforts while you are performing. Interference can come from external sources, such as environmental conditions. Or its source can be inside you, as in the case of fatigue, anxiety, or fear. Whether the interference you face is external or internal, the best way to overcome it is by embracing the mindset of a champion and not letting it get the upper hand.

Luck refers to the fluctuations in your performance that are simply due to chance. In the game of golf, balls land in divots in the middle of a fairway, they bounce off marker stakes and stay in bounds, and they even miraculously skip across water hazards and come to rest back on land. In business, too, we are sometimes lucky enough to be in the right place at the right time, or unfortunate to be in the wrong place at the wrong one. Nevertheless, bad luck and good luck are shared by all and tend to balance out over the long haul.

In sum, understanding the influence that talent, interference, and luck have on performance is vital to maintaining a healthy mental perspective in business and in life. First and foremost, people who want to succeed must attain a high level of talent, by making significant commitments of time and effort. Then, interference must be monitored and managed during competition. Individuals must take the time to identify the sources of interference that most affect their performance and embrace the mindset of a champion to deal with them.

Luck is simply that—luck. Remember, all business has its ups and downs.

Sounds a lot like business these days, doesn't it? Doing more with less, poor market conditions, commoditization of our products, new competitors entering the business every day. Adversity is ever-present in business life, to one degree or another. There will always be winners and losers, leaders and followers, and those climbing to the top while others are heading toward the bottom. Your ability to thrive on adversity—or at least to take it in stride—can make an enormous difference in the outcome you achieve.

> IT IS SIMPLE TO BE MENTALLY SHARP WHEN WE ARE DOING WELL. THE REAL TEST COMES DURING TIMES OF ADVERSITY.

As we discussed a moment ago, the first key to dealing with adversity lies in your ability to view the situation with the right frame of mind. Take another example from the world of golf. Imagine that you have to make a five-foot putt on the 18th hole to win the match and your partner has just anxiously reminded you of how much is at stake. How would you view this situation? Would you perceive it from a position of fear (and possibly a little irritation) or one of opportunity? To a tour pro, there wouldn't be any question. That five-foot putt would be an opportunity, pure and simple.

From a mental toughness point of view, I have to admit that tour pros are pretty abnormal. That's right, "abnormal"—they don't think and react like the "norm." When presented with difficult conditions, normal people experience self-doubt, anxiety, pressure, and fear of being embarrassed. The tour pro has learned to keep those emotions in check and see adversity as at least neutral and possibly even a positive.

Photo by Al Tielemans, *Sports Illustrated*

"That's what we are waiting for—to have that opportunity on Sunday to compete
for the greatest title against some of the best players in the world.
I would love that opportunity!" —*Phil Mickelson*

Prior to winning the 2004 Masters Championship at Augusta National, Phil Mickelson was tagged with the title of "Best Player Never to Have Won a Major" — a distinction no player on the PGA Tour is likely to have envied. When he was asked how he would handle the intimidating prospect of being paired with Tiger Woods in the final group on the last day of the Masters, Phil responded, "That's what we are waiting for—to have that opportunity on Sunday to compete for the greatest title against some of the best players in the world. I would love that opportunity!"

Adversity can be a good thing in that it gives a player the opportunity to see how well he or she can respond to a challenge— and maybe even show off a little. And even if it isn't a good thing, it isn't necessarily a bad one. It is merely the reality of the situation— an obstacle that must be dealt with and overcome.

These moments of adversity also give a player the opportunity to practice mental toughness skills. The best time to train mental skills is when your game (or your business) is not at its best. It is simple to be mentally sharp when we are doing well. The real test comes during times of adversity. Adversity pushes the limits of our mental toughness skills and provides us with the opportunity to move to the next level— even if we don't always recognize it at the time.

Play the Game

What do playing in one of golf's major championships, selling a product to a top prospect, and providing world-class service all have in common? They each involve a period of learning followed by performance. As with all performance-oriented activities, golf and business require the performer first to learn the necessary technical skills and then to "play the game" by executing these skills under real-life conditions. Taking it to the course requires that individuals shift from a learn-the-game to a play-the-game mentality.

Obviously, a key to excelling in any competitive endeavor is the ability to develop a high level of technical skills that can be called upon during competition. The better your skills, the greater are your chances of success.

But in order to take it to the course, we have to stop learning and apply what we have learned. We must take the time to play the game and, in fact, enjoy doing it. There's a reason we call it *playing* a game instead of *executing* a game or *accomplishing* a game, or whatever.

Peak performers report time and again that during competition they simply perform with little attention to how they are accomplishing that performance. Michael Jordan didn't worry about the position of his hand on the ball while shooting a three-pointer, Roger Federer is not concerned with the position of his feet while playing a tie-breaker in the fifth set, and Annika Sorenstam isn't worried about whether her swing looks technically correct while playing golf. Top performers are not distracted by these things while they're competing.

By the time you take it to the course, you want to feel comfortable with the skills and routines that you have established in your training, and simply view the game as an opportunity to demonstrate your skills. Tiger Woods said, "I just set up and I just go. I don't feel like I'm trying to put more weight on the balls of my feet, more weight on my right side or left side. I just get to a position where I feel comfortable and whatever shot I want to play I will play by feel."

To champions like Woods, practice periods are the time to refine and master skills, while playing periods are the time to go out there and make it happen.

To effectively play your game—whatever that game might be—you must quiet your mind and put aside your interest in further

CONTROL THE CONTROLLABLE

When I study what great players do to answer the door when opportunity knocks, one theme emerges over and over again: They strive to control the controllable, not the outcome.

"I was shaking in my boots, obviously," PGA Tour rookie Ben Curtis admitted after winning the 2003 British Open. "But I was just out there very focused on what I had to do and I let my work speak for itself. And if it was good enough, fine. If not, I can live with it."

The ability to live with the results of their efforts, good or bad, helps top golfers approach a situation of great magnitude (like being in contention in a major championship) as an opportunity. If players instead perceive such a situation as a threat—focusing on the threat of failing, choking, embarrassment, or of never getting another chance—the situation can get the best of them.

In the heat of battle, Curtis, up to that point the 396th-ranked pro golfer in the world, controlled the things that were under his control: his effort, his decisions, his reactions, and his emotions. He knew he couldn't control the eventual outcome.

That would depend on many things beyond his control, including how the rest of the field played, how the weather cooperated during his time on the course, whether his ball landed in a divot when it hit the fairway, and how often the wind gusted while his ball was airborne.

But he controlled everything he could, and as a result Curtis became the first player to win a major championship on his first try since 1913.

In business, too, there are things you can control, and things you can't. In the first group are the time and effort you put into your work and the skills and training you bring to it. Additionally, you can control how you behave in your work environment, how you interact with colleagues, and how you treat customers. Controlling those actions and reactions that are within your control while at work can take some of the sting out of those conditions that you can't control.

Among the many factors you cannot control in your work environment are company politics, the state of the economy, and your budget. Although these factors may be out of your control, how you deal with them is not.

Ask yourself the following questions:

- *Do I control what I can to the best of my ability and then accept the result, good or bad?*
- *Do I recognize the issues that are out of my control and avoid getting drawn into discussions and conflicts that involve these things?*

How do you respond when something out of your control has a negative impact on your business results? Do you beat yourself up over it, or do you let it go, learn from it, and move on? Champions focus their energy on the essential drivers of their results, the drivers that they can control. As to those they can't, Tiger Woods once put it this way:

"That's just in the lap of the golfing gods. Sometimes they're looking upon you in a good way, and other times they say, 'You know what? You're not getting it this time.' That's just part of playing the game. You're going to get good breaks, and you'll get bad ones, but if you just keep hanging in there, keep grinding, keep working on your game, eventually you're going to get some breaks to go your way."

developing your skills. By doing that, you will allow your mind and body to automatically run the skills that you have established during training. This is what athletes refer to as playing "in the zone." The more you clutter your mind or become overly concerned with how you are performing, or how you are executing a skill, the less likely you will perform freely and on automatic pilot.

Here are a number of suggestions for you to consider in improving your ability to play your game:

1. Create on-the-job training activities where you can blend learning and playing. Be selective, but choose certain work situations where you can try to push the transfer of new skills consciously while performing in real-life situations.

2. Define other work situations in which you will cease learning and focus all of your attention on the performance itself. Allow yourself to be natural and perform automatically without attempting to consciously control the technical aspects of your skill.

3. Identify a specific time each month (such as the first Monday) that you will stop and evaluate your performance and the reasons for both your good and not-so-good results. Suspend judgment and evaluation while performing—allow yourself the opportunity to focus only on performing your skills as opposed to "fixing" your faults.

As you learn to truly *play* the game, you will begin to view business situations as opportunities to have fun and enjoy displaying the talents that you have worked so hard to develop. Avoid that crippling final-exam mentality of "I hope I'm ready. I hope I don't forget anything. I wish I'd had more time to prepare." That judgmental mindset suppresses the creative, expressive energy that you will rely on to successfully play the game.

Step #2: Turn best practices into routines.

For most of us, the word "routine" conjures up images of boring, repetitive tasks. For the athlete, however, the word takes on a far more important meaning. Routines are one of their best-kept secrets.

In 2002, I was working with players on the U.S. team as they competed for the Solheim Cup at the Interlachen Country Club in Edina, Minnesota. The Solheim Cup, like the men's Ryder Cup, is the event in which the top 12 women golfers from the United States compete against the top 12 women from Europe. On the final day, after the U.S. team had won and received the cup during the closing ceremonies, I was walking to the shuttle that would take us back to the hotel, where the teams later gather and enjoy one another's camaraderie.

It was about two o'clock in the afternoon and I was walking past the driving range when I noticed a lone figure down there. It was Terry McNamara, Annika Sorenstam's caddy. Everyone else was gone, or in the process of leaving, and he was standing there, holding her bag next to a stack of balls.

I just had to go over and ask him, "Terry, what are you still doing here?"

And he said, "I'm waiting for Annika. We're going to work on some things. It's still light out, and whenever we finish a tournament round, if we teed up in the morning we use the afternoon for practice. That's just our routine. We never break the rule. We'll get to the party, but after dark."

Now what's interesting to me about this anecdote isn't that Sorenstam likes to practice after a tournament or even that she views the presence of light as a signal to practice. What I find instructive is what she does relative to her competition. Again, remember that this was the Solheim Cup. The players at this event represented the top 12 from the U.S. and the same number from Europe, 24 world-

Photo by Darren Carroll, *Sports Illustrated*

"I wanted a challenge, something that would push me a little harder
and take my game to the next level." —*Annika Sorenstam*

class champions in all. And how many of these players were on the driving range following the event? Just one.

Annika Sorenstam's willingness to maintain these disciplined practice routines that go far beyond even those of her nearest competitors is undoubtedly one reason she has been so dominant on the LPGA Tour. Her post-round practice routine is simply one example. Imagine the disciplined routines that she follows in other aspects of her life: fitness, nutrition, instruction, travel, pre-round warm-up, practice rounds, and everything else.

Champions like Sorenstam are always looking to develop the routines that will take their game to the next level. In 2003, Annika accepted the challenge of competing against the men on the PGA Tour at the Colonial, the first woman to do so since 1958. Why? In her own words: "I wanted to see if my game could hold up against the best male players in the world, to see if I could play their courses. I wanted a challenge, something that would push me a little harder and take my game to the next level."

Last year, I had the opportunity to work with the Cooke Financial Group of Wachovia Securities in Indianapolis, Indiana. The Cooke Group is a champion in the financial services industry. They have been recognized consistently by *Barron's* magazine as one of the Top 100 Financial Advisors in the country and in 2006, were ranked #2 in America among *Research* magazine's list of Top-Ranked Family Teams.

As we discussed the reasons for their success, Chris and Brian Cooke immediately pointed to the team's ability to turn best practices into routines. They explained that their business is first and foremost a service industry, and like similar industries, the client experience is essential. They didn't leave the client experience to chance—hoping that just because they staffed their team with competent, well-intentioned professionals, client service would take care of itself.

COOKE FINANCIAL GROUP
CLIENT EXPERIENCE MODEL
(New Accounts and Referrals)

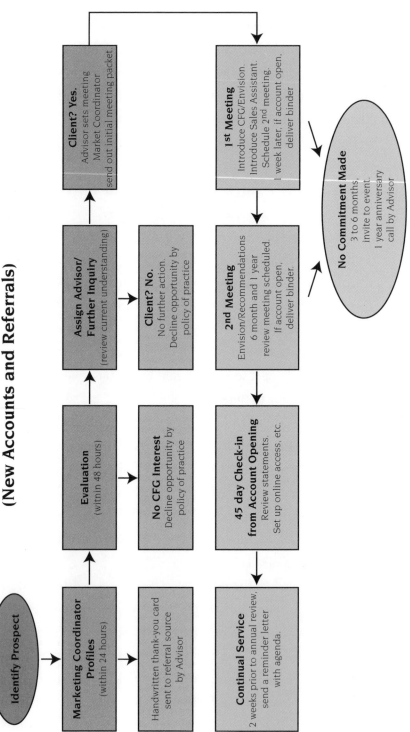

Instead, the Cooke Group has developed and implemented a unique Client Experience Model, a process that all members of the team routinely follow.

The Cookes' Client Experience Model was not an optional, guiding philosophy that they aspired to achieve. It was a well-defined behavioral routine that they followed to ensure consistency, quality, and exceptional service for each of their clients. On the opposite page is a flow chart of the routine that they follow for new accounts and referrals.

Each step in the model demonstrates the Cooke Group's commitment to turning best practices into routines. Note how action-oriented and time-specific each step is. Even more impressive was the Cooke Group's willingness to reflect on and improve the things that they were not doing. As with Tiger Woods, the Cooke Group knew what it took to be top in their industry yet continued to measure where they stood relative to other top advisory teams across the country.

As we discussed what they needed to do to take their practice to the next level, we agreed that an even better approach would be for them to deliver their client services as a coordinated team, rather than having separate specialists work in silos to perform their various functions.

So what did they do? They completely revamped their compensation system to reward team members for team behavior. They defined how each team member would contribute to servicing and adding value to the client, and integrated the defined responsibilities into their service and prospecting systems. In other words, they turned best practices into systemic business processes that have become part of the infrastructure of their practice.

Recall our discussion of Tiger Woods' willingness to continually evaluate and refine what he does. In business, the Cooke Group exemplifies this same ability to measure where they stand, train like champions, and take it to the course. They will not allow themselves to be shackled by the adage, "if it ain't broke, don't fix it." Champions simply don't think that way. Champions understand that they must continue to improve, never stand still, and thrive on the opportunity to take their business to the next level.

Turning best practices into routines is not a simple task. It is much easier to write about than it is to do. And frankly, even writing about it isn't that easy. As I've worked on this book, I've struggled with setting aside the time and energy to turn the practice of book writing into a disciplined routine. There are just so many interests that are high priority—playing with my kids, spending time with my wife, meeting with clients, giving seminars, producing training materials, and all the rest. I'm sure that there are areas in your life where you would like to be more disciplined, but every time you try to do something about it, you get sidetracked.

Here's a thought: Many of us would be more effective (and far less crazed) if we simply stopped trying to be great at so many things. If you're a perpetual self-improver—the kind of person who finds himself or herself embracing a new and different best practice practically every month, maybe you'd do better to select one best practice and master it. That was Arnold Palmer's lesson from his father: Stick to something long enough to master it.

Remember the Lay's potato chip commercial with the slogan, "Bet you can't eat just one"? That expression applies to the way many of us pursue self-improvement. Like golfers trying to master the game by experimenting with the most recently published swing tip (and next month, a new tip), businesspeople often attempt to implement a new best practice, lose interest before they've really mastered it, and then move on to something else.

Champions, however, develop an ability to identify a best

Photo by James Drake, *Sports Illustrated*

"When I'd practice at California Club in San Francisco,
I would visualize holes at Augusta." —*Ken Venturi*

practice that is worthy of their time, and then they stick with it long enough to turn it into a routine. It becomes a part of who they are and what they do, not just one more potato chip from the bag.

I remember a conversation I had with CBS's lead golf analyst, Ken Venturi, about his days as a top golfer. In Venturi's prime, driving ranges as we know them today were practically nonexistent. Players would hit balls to a person, a "shagger," who would shag, or fetch, the balls and return them to the player to be hit again.

Venturi's routine was to use his shagger to help him imagine the holes that he'd soon be playing. "When I'd practice at California Club in San Francisco, I would visualize holes at Augusta," Venturi recalled. "I would put my shagger in a little cove to the left and draw it into him. Then, I'd put him in a little cove on the right, and I'd fade it into him. Then, when I got to a hole that I had to draw the ball, I'd visualize my caddie sitting right in that cove, and there it goes." Following this routine, Venturi was able to condition himself to feel comfortable hitting the shot each hole required.

The key to turning best practices into routines is to select one best practice worthy of routine-status and master it. I ask my clients to convert one per year—that's it, just one. Forming routines takes time, energy, focus, support, and intention. Attempting to spread these resources over a number of best practices diffuses the business's ability to truly master any of them.

For you high achievers who think, "What—only one? I can take on more than one," feel free to give it a shot. However, if you struggle to form disciplined routines in your professional or personal life, it's often better to simplify your effort and focus on one. Form just one essential routine per year for the next five years and you will be amazed by the results.

Stop for a moment and consider the areas of your life, professional or personal, that you would like to make more systematic, more routine. Jot down one—that's right, only one—that you are willing to turn into a routine.

For example, you might decide to create a routine of networking with two new business contacts each month. Next, ask yourself if you know anyone who has already been successful at doing something like that. Set up a time to meet and find out more about how he or she did it. Take notes as to what barriers had to be overcome and what the other person did to stay motivated. Finally, create an action plan with due dates of the specific behaviors that you will implement to turn your identified best practice into a routine. Stick with this process until you have formed a new habit!

CONVERTING BEST PRACTICES INTO ROUTINES

Future routine:

_____

_____

_____

Individuals to consult: Meeting dates:

_____   _____

_____   _____

_____   _____

Insights from these meetings:

_____

_____

_____

_____

Steps to turning this best practice into a routine:

	Action		Due date:
Step 1:	_____		_____
Step 2:	_____		_____
Step 3:	_____		_____

Step #3: Take action, now!

Identifying and prioritizing the key factors that will take your business performance to the next level will not change your results all by themselves. Pursuing training and organizational development to improve in these essential areas won't bring you immediate results either.

Instead, you have to take action—now. You have to establish an action plan that ensures that all anticipated improvements are integrated into your business operation. This action plan should define specifically how and when these improvements will be introduced into your business. Assign deadlines to each item on your action plan. Make them realistic, but once you've established them, stick to them.

As soon as a plan is in place, champions are willing to put it to the test. Rather than second-guess their plan or overanalyze its merits, they get on with it. Why hire an architect to create plans for a beautiful home and then never build it?

LPGA veteran Meg Mallon once told me that she rarely passed up an opportunity to put her skills to the test. She wanted to know that they would be there when she most needed them. "Even in tournaments, I would say 'I'm practicing this putt for the U.S. Open,'" Meg recalled. "I'd actually practice in tournaments—becoming what I thought was a better player for a more important situation. . . .

When you see yourself taking the risk in a tough situation and pulling it off, you just really build your confidence."

Champions do not want to sit around at a later date and ask themselves, "I wonder what would have happened if only I had done such-and-such?" Instead, they take action. They know it is the execution of the plan that produces results, not the plan itself.

I often hear people say that Tiger Woods was born to be a champion, as if his success was somehow inevitable; quite the contrary. I'm sure Woods would argue that he has taken certain actions that his counterparts have not—from hitting hundreds of thousands of balls, to working out, to sacrificing more than most people would be willing to give up to achieve his desired goal.

> **TALENT IS DEVELOPED THROUGH HARD WORK, QUALITY INSTRUCTION, AND DELIBERATE PRACTICE.**

The research is very clear in this area: Talent is developed through hard work, quality instruction, and deliberate practice. Although certain physiological and genetic factors might contribute to an athlete's potential (such as swing arc, body type, and height), the fulfillment of that potential is directly linked to actions taken by the athlete.

Step #4: Establish accountability for results

Creating an action plan without assigning responsibility for its implementation would be the equivalent of getting a road map to a destination from A.A.A. or Mapquest but having no one to drive the car. Once you have established what you intend to improve, how you intend to improve it, and when you will start implementing, make sure that all individuals involved are accountable for their respective roles.

PREPARE OTHERS FOR THE NEW AND IMPROVED

If you are making improvements to existing ways of doing things, your changes may not affect you alone. There may be others involved who need to know that things are changing in your business. As you plan to take your newly improved skills or processes *to the course* and put them to use, make sure that you have considered others who need to know what's going on.

Years ago, I was retained by a company to provide training for several departments on the topic of Total Quality Management (TQM), a continuous-improvement philosophy based in part on the work of the American statistician W. Edwards Deming. The company pulled its staff out of the field to sit in a classroom for several days to learn the theory of TQM and consider how it could be applied in their work environment.

The people who attended these sessions were enthusiastic, engaged, and committed to the learning process. When I next visited the company several months later I met with some of the attendees and asked how they were doing with applying the TQM strategies we'd discussed. They told me that although they had enjoyed the training they found themselves unable to transfer it to their work environment. When I asked them why, one quickly responded, "Because our managers don't have a clue about what we're talking about. They weren't at the training."

The frustrated staff members couldn't have been more right. Once I had been invited by the human resources department to conduct the training, I should have made sure that all levels of the organization would be represented in the room. I mistakenly assumed that the managers must be on board, if not already trained. I later learned that the managers didn't feel that they needed to be trained in TQM, or even really understand it, because they believed it could simply be implemented by their staffers. By not preparing everyone to understand and use the TQM process, the organization had failed to get the most benefit from it. That was one mistake I never made again.

Have you ever made a mistake like that? For example, have you ever tried to make a significant change in your work or personal life and then met with unexpected resistance from others (such as a manager, colleagues, your spouse, or kids)? Was it because you failed to adequately prepare them for it? So before implementing a plan, consider anyone else who may be affected. Get them on board at the beginning and you'll have cleared a major obstacle from your path.

To do that, ask yourself these two questions:

1. *Who else needs to be involved in or informed about the improvements that I'm planning to make?*

_____

_____

_____

2. *What impact could such changes have on these individuals? What other considerations or accommodations need to be made to ensure that there will be minimal resistance to **taking it to the course**?*

_____

_____

_____

First, you must assign ultimate responsibility for the change to one living, breathing individual. This may be you, someone you are paying, or someone that you have recruited to assume the responsibility. Ask yourself, "If and when this change has a significant impact on business, who will I thank, reward, or recognize?" On the other hand, if the change never occurs, or does not have the anticipated effect on results, ask yourself, "Who is ultimately responsible and what will the consequences be?"

If you have no one but yourself to hold accountable, you may have to strive extra hard to overcome procrastination. One strategy I've seen work is to partner with a colleague who is also embarking on an improvement plan. Agree to hold each other accountable for the implementation of your respective plans. Turn it into a bet— dinner, tickets to a sporting event, or some other prize for the person who does the best job of taking it to the course.

I spend a substantial amount of time each year consulting with sales teams to increase their effectiveness. In particular, I've worked with a number of wholesaling teams from financial-product firms to develop and implement programs, such as business management strategies, for the financial advisors through whom they distribute their products. The wholesalers rely on these programs to deliver additional value to the financial advisors and the advisors' clients— with the ultimate goal of creating a long-term win-win-win relationship that helps drive sales. The logic is that if the wholesaler can deliver a product that is right for the client and a value-added program that is right for the advisor, then all parties win—an improved financial portfolio for the client, a more efficient and productive business for the advisor, and increased sales for the wholesaler.

However, for the wholesaler to receive the benefit of increased sales, he or she must do more than show up with financial products and value-added programs. These tangibles do not sell themselves. They must be sold. The wholesaler has to gain access to the appropriate advisors, present a compelling value proposition, understand an advisor's business, and execute the sales process to completion.

In the world of sales, just as in the world of sports, results are essential. Salespeople, like athletes, are accountable for their results.

YES, WINNING MATTERS.

Having products, value-added programs, and sales processes means nothing if they are not leveraged, positioned, and applied with one goal in mind: to produce sales. Champions in any competitive arena understand that they must demonstrate the relationship between effort and results.

Champions want to win—badly! That doesn't mean they'll do absolutely anything in order to win. Champions have ethics, morals, and character. They play within the rules, enjoy success, accept defeat, and shake hands with their opponents after a tough competition.

How badly do you want to win? Are you willing to sacrifice certain conveniences and commit valuable time and energy to doing what it takes to win? Champions don't simply show up for work to collect a paycheck. They show up with the objective of working on the things that get them one step closer to winning—a major championship, a Super Bowl, a Stanley Cup, a sales competition, a bonus, or a critical piece of business. Yes, winning matters.

ONE FINAL ESSENTIAL: START ALL OVER AGAIN!

As I'm sure you know by now, becoming a top performer in any field is not a one-shot deal but an on-going, never-ending process. If you truly want to become the best at what you do, you will find that you are never satisfied with your results and that you will always want to achieve more, which brings us back to the diagram.

Once you have completed one cycle of Define Your Goal…Know What It Takes…Measure Where You Stand…Train Like a Champion…and Take It to the Course, you can start the entire process all over again. Each journey around the cycle is equivalent to moving up one rung on your Slinky of success. Enjoy it. It is a rewarding and lifelong process.

CHAPTER 7

USE IT BEFORE YOU LOSE IT

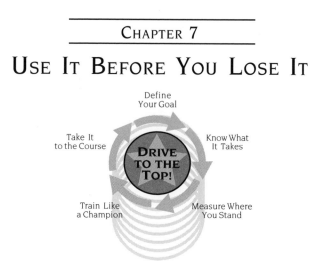

ABOUT 10 YEARS AGO, ON CHRISTMAS MORNING, my brother-in-law proudly presented me with a gift. As I unwrapped it, I discovered that it was a golf item, a putter to be exact. However, it was not just any putter, it was an orange and blue putter. Now for you non-Gator fans out there, I should tell you that I, my wife, and my brother-in-law are all University of Florida alumni. And if you are a Florida Gator, no two colors go together as well as orange and blue. That goes for bumper stickers, bath towels, T-shirts, baby clothes, throw blankets, billiard balls, and yes, even putters!

As I was stowing away my Christmas gifts at the end of the day, I recall grabbing the putter and thinking, "I better not put this in my golf bag—it's sure to get scratched. I think I'll save it for a *special occasion.*" So I put it where I figured it would be safe.

Flash forward to 2007. The two previous years had been phenomenal for us Florida Gators. We'd won back-to-back national championships in basketball (2006 and 2007) and a national championship in football (2006), as well. Shortly after the crowning of the national champion Gator basketball team in '07, I was off to my annual golf boondoggle with about 10 of my non-Gator friends. The *special occasion* had arrived!

I had it all planned in my head. On the first hole, when I was about to putt, instead of pulling out my old faithful Ping Anser putter, I'd proudly whip out my mint condition, orange and blue Gator putter. Of course, I'd accompany each made putt with a Gator chomp (arms extended straight out in front of you, opening and closing, simulating the jaws of Gator). Could it get any better?

Just one problem: I had lost the putter. As I searched through my house, closets, garage, attic, anywhere a putter could fit, I couldn't find it. We had moved residences twice in the last 10 years, and who knows where it ended up. I had learned my lesson—use it before you lose it!

So let's talk about this book. If you found value in it, USE IT BEFORE YOU LOSE IT! Believe me, I'm not trying to increase your perceived value of this book. Frankly, the book before you opened it was far less valuable than it is now that you have read it and put some work into it. The retail value of this book has multiplied many times over in the self-assessments you've completed, the thoughts you've wrestled with, the notes you've taken, and the decisions you've made.

You've taken the time to examine your character and your ability to apply the five essentials of champions to your individual circumstances. With all of that effort being behind you at this point, the one factor that will ultimately determine whether this book has any real value is *the action that you take*!

So let me say it one more time: USE IT BEFORE YOU LOSE IT. The IT in this case is much more than the book itself. IT includes your knowledge, your insights, your plans, your intentions. IT is the reason you read this book. Without IT, the book has little value!

So before you place this book on a shelf, possibly to never be picked up again, stop and ask yourself "What will I do with IT?"

What one or two specific actions will you take immediately to ensure that there is a realized return on your investment? If you need to, go back and review the notes that you've made throughout this book, and highlight those that you consider to be most essential. Now, turn to the back of this book, specifically the page facing the back cover. Here you will find your personal "Post-It Note." On this note, write down what you WILL do, not what you hope to do.

Lastly, place this book in a visible location on your desk, in your office, on your nightstand, or anywhere else you are likely to see it often. Let it serve as a constant reminder of what you will achieve. Now, commit to this—open the book daily to your personal Post-It Note, read the actions that you've committed to, and get them done. Shelve the book when, and only when, you've completed these actions.

This is how champions behave. Champions identify what's essential and then take action. Champions create their own destiny. You can, too. And when you do, you will DRIVE TO THE TOP!

GLOSSARY
Golf Terms for the Non-Golfer

Many of the golf terms used in this book are probably familiar to readers, golfers or not. Here are some that may not be:

Approach shots are the shots that players hit from the fairway or the rough in an attempt to land the ball on the green.

Chipping refers to a short-game shot taken from off the green, usually within five yards from the fringe of a green, with a club other than a putter. A chip typically is designed to roll farther than it flies.

Greens in regulation is a measurement of the average number of greens per round that a player reaches in two shots less than the par for that hole.

Hole-Out refers to a shot in golf, hit from off of the putting surface, that ends up in the hole.

Lip-out refers to a putt that hits the edge of the hole and does not go in.

Par is a number assigned to each hole (typically three, four, or five) that corresponds to its distance and difficulty. For pro golfers, par is the expected standard for each hole. An "eagle" is a score of two shots less than par. A "birdie" is a score of one shot less than par. A "bogey" is a score of one shot more than par. A "double-bogey" is a score of two shots more than par.

Pitching refers to a short-game shot typically taken from five to 50 yards from the fringe of a green. A pitch typically is a high arcing shot designed to fly farther than it rolls. A "pitch and run" is the term for a pitch shot that rolls farther than it flies.

Putt refers to a shot hit once a player is on the putting green, where the player attempts to roll the ball along the surface of the green into the hole.

Putts per Green in Regulation is a measurement of the average number of putts required for a player to get the ball in the hole (after the player has landed the ball on the putting surface).

Scoring average is the calculation of a golfer's average score for 18 holes over an extended period of time.

Scrambling refers to a player's ability (measured as a percentage of opportunities) to make a score of par on a hole after having missed the green in regulation.

Total Driving is a measurement of a golfer's ability to drive the golf ball from the tee. It is calculated through a weighted formula that combines two skills: (1) how far a player drives the ball and (2) how accurately a player drives a ball.

Up and down refers to getting the ball into the hole in two shots, starting from off the green.

What I Will Do With "IT"